Yorkshire's North West Frontier

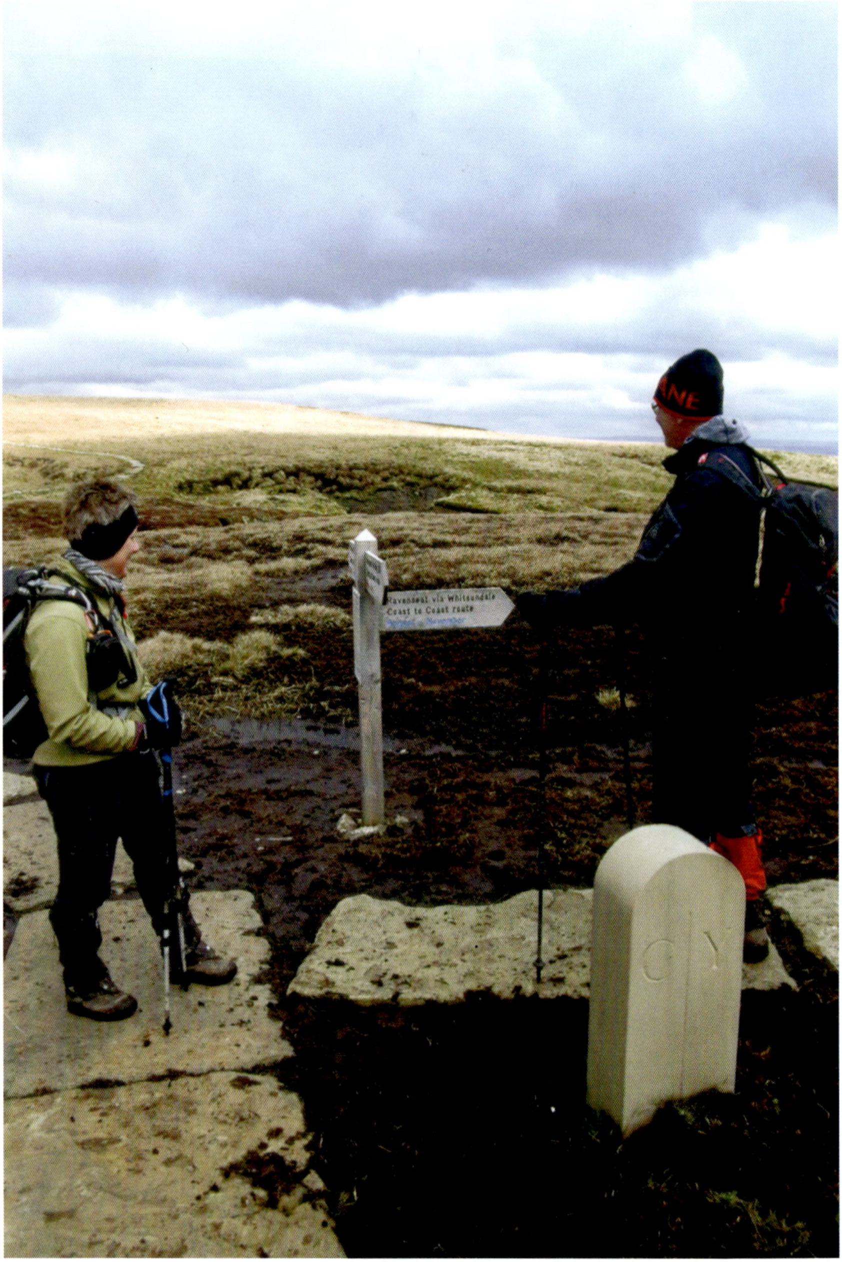
Ravenseat via Whitsundale
Coast to Coast route

Yorkshire's North West Frontier

Walking the Old County Boundary

TERRY ASHBY

To Alan and Holly
Good Walking!
Enjoy!
Terry
2019

HAYLOFT

First published in Great Britain by Hayloft Publishing Ltd, 2019

© Terry Ashby, 2019
All illustrations © Terry Ashby except Lapwing & Spring Gentian painting © Judith Owston

The right of Terry Ashby to be identified as the Author of the Work has been asserted by him in accordance with the Copyright, Designs and Patents Act 1988

All rights reserved. Apart from any use permitted under UK copyright law no part of this publication may be reproduced, stored in a retrieval system, or transmitted, in any form or by any means without the prior written permission of the publisher, nor be otherwise circulated in any form of binding or cover other than that in which it is published and without a similar condition being imposed on the subsequent purchaser.

A CIP catalogue record for this book is available from the British Library

ISBN 978-1-910237-50-2

Designed, printed and bound in the EU

Hayloft policy is to use papers that are natural, renewable and recyclable products and made from wood grown in sustainable forests. The logging and manufacturing processes are expected to conform to the environmental regulations of the country of origin.

Hayloft Publishing Ltd,
a company registered in England number 4802586
2 Staveley Mill Yard, Staveley, Kendal, LA8 9LR (registered office)
L'Ancien Presbytère, 21460 Corsaint, France (editorial office)

Email: books@hayloft.eu
Tel: 07971 352473

www.hayloft.eu

This book is printed with the offset of carbon emissions and support for
Forest Protection, Pará, Brazil

Climate neutral
Print product
ClimatePartner.com/12667-1905-1002

Frontispiece: *Walkers on the frontier, inspecting the new installations on Nine Standards Rigg.*

To all true Tykes - those still living in

God's Own County

and those in exile elsewhere;

And to the Memory of William Thomas Palmer,

'A Man Before His Time'

Contents

List of Illustrations	8
Acknowledgements	10
Sketch Map of the North-West Frontier and Surrounding Area	12
Introduction	13
William Thomas Palmer, 1877-1954	18
Yorkshire as a County	24
Cauldron Snout to Mickle Fell Summit	33
Mickle Fell Summit to Ley Seat	42
Ley Seat to Stainmore Summit	48
Stainmore Summit to Tan Hill	53
Tan Hill	61
Tan Hill to Nine Standards Rigg – the Lyell-Hothfield Boundary Dispute	70
Tan Hill to Nine Standards Rigg – the Route	76
The Nine Standards	83
Nine Standards Rigg to Aisgill Summit – the Mallerstang Valley	90
Aisgill Summit to Rawthey Bridge	102
Rawthey Bridge to the River Lune – the Howgills	112
Conclusion – Putting It All Together	125
Updates	130
Bibliography, References and Further Reading	131
Useful Websites	134

Illustrations

Frontispiece: Walkers on the frontier, inspecting the new installations on Nine Standards Rigg	2
Map, the 'North West Frontier' and surrounding area	12
William Palmer as a young man	21
The start of the North-West Frontier – Maize Beck joins the River Tees below Cauldron Snout – Cow Green dam visible above – that dam' wall	33
Lapwing and Spring Gentian – from a painting by Judith Owston, Middleton-in-Teesdale	36
Isolated Birkdale Farm – the Pennine Way runs past the house	38
Mickle Fell from the north-west – Maize Beck in the foreground	39
Numbered boundary stone by Maize Beck	40
Making a point on Mickle Fell summit	42
Inscription above the doorway of the former school and chapel Grains o' th' Beck	45
North Riding milestone, Grains o' th' Beck – 'Brough 7 Middleton 7¼'	46
Rey Cross, Stainmore	54
Trackbed of the former Stainmore Railway near Ay Gill	57
Replica sign on Stainmore Summit – the original was removed to the National Railway Museum in York	58
The former Barras Station House overlooking the Eden Valley	59
The world-famous Tan Hill Inn, highest pub in Britain	63
Swaledale sheep – found everywhere in the Pennines	65
Boundary stone on the Barras-Tan Hill road	69
'LH 1912' – Lord Hothfield's boundary stone on Cocklake Rigg	70
The hamlet of Ravenseat on the Coast to Coast Walk	77
Ravenseat – the packhorse bridge over Whitsundale Beck	79
Eighteenth century Smardale Bridge over Scandale Beck – a long way from the county boundary but once the site of an inn, reputedly a meeting-place of the Kaber Rigg Plotters	81
A few of the Nine Standards – Mickle Fell on the far horizon	85

ILLUSTRATIONS

Nine Standards Rigg on a good day – the eroded peat before the slabs were laid	87
Boundary stone near Hollow Mill Cross – 'Hamlet of Birkdale County of York'	91
Approaching Wild Boar Fell, Mallerstang	93
The cairns on Wild Boar Fell and the view south along the Mallerstang Valley	94
Hell Gill Force, Mallerstang	95
The ruins of High Dyke, once a drovers' inn, on the High Way	96
The Watercut, Mary Bourne's sculpture on the High Way	97
The ruins of Pendragon Castle, Mallerstang	99
Statue of Ruswarp, the heroic and faithful Border Collie, on Garsdale Station	104
Swarth Fell Pike – the 'triple junction' cairn where the North Riding, the West Riding and Westmorland meet – Baugh Fell in the background	106
West Riding-North Riding boundary stone and milestone below the railway bridge, Garsdale Head	107
The Cross Keys Inn, Cautley – no booze here!	108
The view north east along the Rawthey Valley	109
The upper cascades of Cautley Spout, highest above-ground waterfall in England	110
Fell ponies – a frequent sight in the Howgills although these are in the North Pennines near High Cup	113
Herdwick sheep – a traditional Lakeland breed but seen here in the Howgills near Cautley	114
Summit of the Calf, highest point in the Howgills	115
The rolling, airy ridges of the Howgills	117
The Howgills – Black Force, Carlin Gill – a fearsome scramble!	118
Carlingill Beck near the bridge	121
Carlingill Bridge	122
Carlingill Beck joins the River Lune – the end of the 'North West Frontier'!	125
The other North-West Frontier – the author on the Karakoram Highway near China's border with Pakistan.	135

Acknowledgements

Many people have helped in many ways in the research and preparation of this book and I extend my grateful thanks to them all:

To the staff of the County Record Offices in Kendal, Durham and Northallerton who dealt with my initially very broad and vague enquiries and quickly gave me leads to follow; also for their permission to quote from documents in their archives; to the staff of various public libraries in Cumbria, North Yorkshire and County Durham for suggesting and acquiring relevant books and for assisting when my very limited computer skills proved hopelessly inadequate; to David Butterworth, Chief Executive of the Yorkshire Dales National Park, and his staff for information on the National Park boundary and for allowing me to see past correspondence; to Adrian Braddy, Editor of *The Dalesman*, for permission to quote from the poem which appeared in its pages many years ago; to Stephen Walker, formerly of Kirkby Stephen, Neil Hanson, formerly of the Tan Hill Inn, Sheila Richardson of Workington (biographer of William T. Palmer), the Rt. Hon. The Lord Hothfield, and my old friends Tom Groves and Sue Bays of York and Kris and Sarah Macmillan of Scarborough, all of whom have read parts of the manuscript and provided additional information and made many helpful suggestions.

To Andy Page and Dave Wilson of Wemmergill Estate for permission to use the private track to Mickle Fell; to Andrew Morrow of Birkdale, Margaret Dent of Thringarth, Les Tyson of Leyburn, Simon Wilson and Alastair Lockett of the North Pennines Area of Outstanding Natural Beauty Partnership and Mike Ogden of Durham County Council for valuable information; to the Rev. Jeremy Thompson of St. John Lee, Hexham, for help in locating the grave of Ada Elizabeth Smith; to David and Ann Singleton, Jim Wood, John Langford, Ian Baxter and other Friends of the Settle-Carlisle Line whose guided walks assisted me in exploring the western side of the Pennines; to Grahame Rose of Hunstanworth and Ray Mand of Durham for their support in tackling Carlin Gill and to Grahame's wife Ruth who accompanied us on a subsequent visit to Mickle Fell, and to Sheila

ACKNOWLEDGEMENTS

Richardson for use of the photograph of William T. Palmer

To James Keelaghan, formerly of Alberta and now of Ontario, Canada, for permission to quote from his song *River Run*; to the family of the late Mike Donald, formerly of Skipton, for permission to quote from his song *The Settle to Carlisle Railway*; to Judith Owston of Middleton-in-Teesdale for permission to reproduce her painting of the lapwing and spring gentian; to the two unknown ladies I met near Nine Standards Rigg who first gave me the idea for this book; to Dawn Robertson of Hayloft Publishing for her invaluable assistance in guiding this novice author through the publishing process and seeing the book into print; to the authors of the many works consulted, all of whom are noted in the text and/or listed in the Bibliography.

I have made all reasonable attempts to obtain copyright holders' permission to use their material; where this has not been possible I apologise to the copyright holders and acknowledge their original work; last, but by no means least, to the late William Palmer for his initial inspiration to 'walk the walk' and the Gloucestershire couple who kindly agreed to be photographed for the frontispiece. I have endeavoured to ensure that all information contained in this book is accurate; any errors are my own, as are all opinions expressed.

Terry Ashby, Co. Durham, November 2018

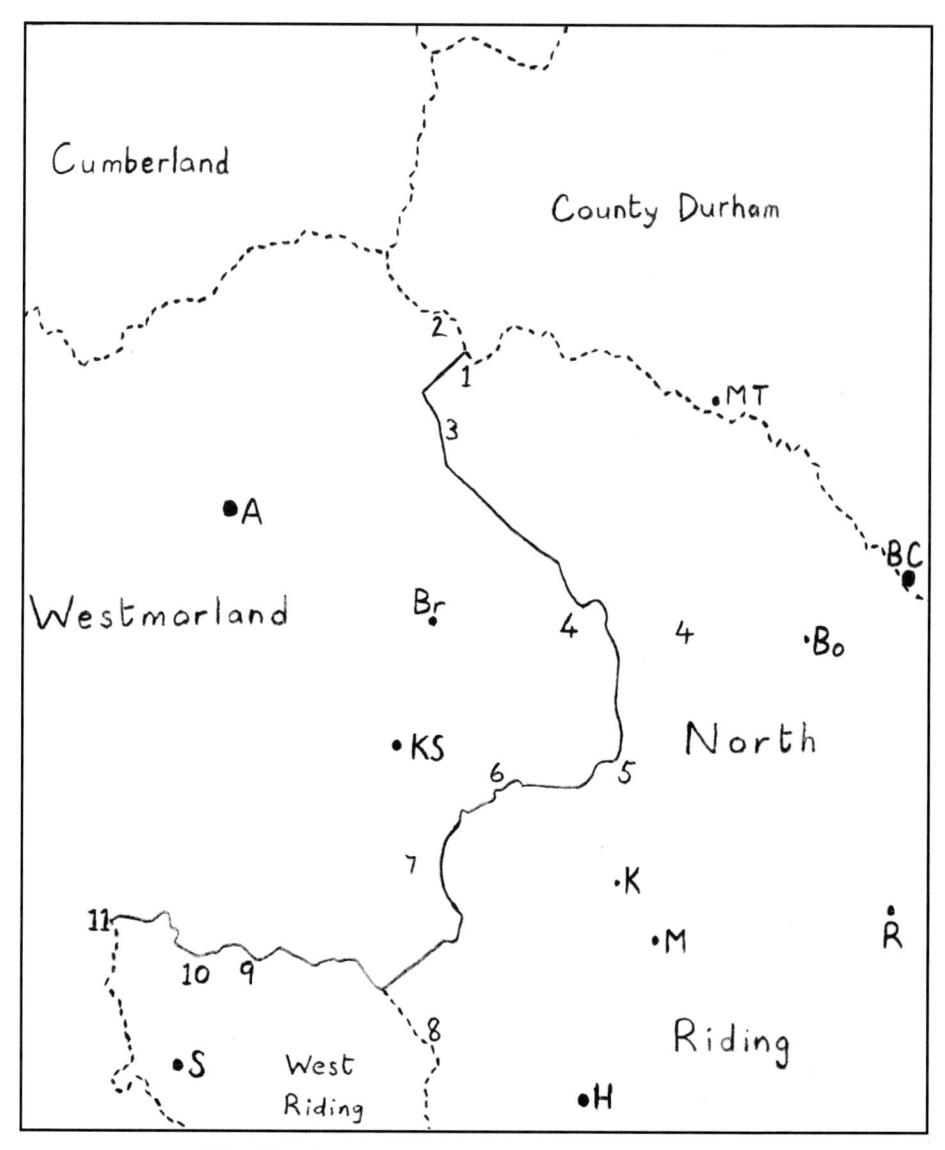

The North-West Frontier and surrounding area.
1 Cauldron Snout; 2 Cow Green; 3 Mickle Fell; 4 Stainmore; 5 Tan Hill; 6 Nine Standards; 7 Mallerstang; 8 Garsdale Head; 9 Cautley Spout; 10 The Calf; 11 Carlingill Bridge.
A Appleby; BC Barnard Castle; Bo Bowes; Br Brough; H Hawes; K Keld; KS Kirkby Stephen; MT Middleton-in-Teesdale; M Muker; R Reeth; S Sedbergh.

Introduction

No coloured cattle graze or ponies run
Upon these moors;
Only the stone-grey sheep
Lie like boulders
On the gentle slopes.

In the early 1960s I moved with my parents from the industrial West Riding to the spectacular Yorkshire coast. In our new home I discovered some back issues of the renowned Yorkshire institution *The Dalesman*. I call it an institution because it's far more than a magazine or even a periodical. The words quoted above are from a poem which appeared in one of those issues and are reproduced here by kind permission of *The Dalesman*. They are all I can remember, I can't remember who wrote them and the present editor of *The Dalesman* is unable to enlighten me, so if anyone can justifiably lay claim to them I apologise. I use them because as a prologue to this book they can hardly be bettered. Still being able to recall them after more than half a century shows that they must have made a deep and lasting impression, even on an eleven-year-old boy.

It was the dawning of an appreciation of just what a great county Yorkshire is – God's Own, no less – and the beginning of a love affair with its wild and lonely open spaces, its sky-wide vistas, its rugged hills and moors and its deep and winding dales, each with its own distinctive character. I began to explore them.

Today, after all these years, I am still doing so, still making new discoveries, still enjoying new experiences, with much, much more ground yet to cover.

So in 2015 I made a conscious decision to walk the length of the old county boundary between Yorkshire and Westmorland which disappeared following the deplorable and reprehensible destruction of the true counties in 1974. But doing so was not an original idea. Credit for that goes to a man named William Palmer, not a Yorkshireman but the author of a book called *Odd Corners in the Yorkshire Dales*, first published in 1937.[1] In that little volume, a copy of which I've had for many years, he devoted a chapter to an account of his walk along this historic line, calling it Yorkshire's 'wildest boundary'; it has always fascinated me and the more I read about it the more I wanted to tackle it myself, consisting as it does almost entirely of high, remote, bleak, boggy fells and moors – just my sort of country! Throughout its length the boundary is within either the North Pennines Area of Outstanding Natural Beauty or the Yorkshire Dales National Park, neither of which existed when Palmer came this way. In fact he died in 1954, the year of the national park's designation.

This is not a step-by-step walking guide (did I hear someone say 'Hooray!')? The main hazards, of which there are quite a number, will be pointed out and general guidance given but the book will focus largely on the boundary itself and its history, disputes and politics, points of interest, wildlife, conservation and environmental issues, legends, tall tales, personal experiences and the like.

On the way it will introduce you, the reader (and, I hope, fellow wanderer) to a large and varied cast of characters – Celts and Romans, Anglo-Saxons, a Viking chieftain and Norman knights, Royalists and Roundheads, a seventeenth century philanthropic aristocrat, shepherds, gamekeepers and landed gentry, doomed lovers, poets and folk singers, various miscreants, a canny serving-maid, confused Americans and a mysterious Spaniard, Scottish raiders, cattle drovers and packhorse traders, map-makers, lawyers and faceless bureaucrats, lead and coal miners, Victorian engineers, a few well-known politicians, an injured airman and a gun-totin' landlady, a notorious highwayman, a canine hero, old Dales 'worthies' and any number of people whose pleasure it is to walk these wild and awe-inspiring Pennine hills. Some will be only brief acquaintances, others you will get to know quite well; you will find them all fascinating. Above all you will get to know William Palmer, truly 'a man before his time'.

I've used the allusion to the British Empire in India by calling the route the North-West Frontier because in former times that's exactly what it was – an area of untamed uplands where the rule of law rarely applied, where boundaries were defined poorly or not at all and where who owned what was frequently a cause of dispute and conflict. Today by contrast anyone with competent map-reading skills can trace the route. Even this is not

---

1 Palmer, William T., *Odd Corners in the Yorkshire Dales: Rambles, Scrambles, Climbs and Sport,* Skeffington & Son, 2nd edition, 1944.

INTRODUCTION

always necessary as for at least the first half of the walk there is, as there was in Palmer's day, a fence or stream to follow. Having said that I must stress that it is in no way an easy walk. It is generally far from habitation or public roads; except for the Settle to Carlisle railway there is no public transport worth mentioning; distances between access points are long; and the terrain is unrelentingly rough going, with tussock grass, heather, deep peat groughs and hags, steep slopes, stream crossings and some very wet and unpleasant bogs. Only on the first approaches does the route directly follow public rights of way and in only a few other places are there any within reasonable proximity. Much of it is devoid of paths except for the occasional quad track.

There are also two major obstacles which didn't exist in Palmer's time – the Warcop Military Training Area and the traffic on the A66 trunk road (the latter is much the more dangerous). The weather, as in all upland areas, is unpredictable and it is definitely not a place to go alone, at least not without leaving details of the route with someone, which of course is normal practice for any competent hill-walker. Here I must admit to a degree of incompetence from time to time in this respect; on one occasion, which you will read about, it almost cost me dear. In another of his books, *Wanderings in the Pennines* (1951), Palmer draws attention to the conditions the walker may encounter:

> Have I any caution to express? This book deals with elevated, stormy, lonely country, where tracks are few and faint and where the penalty of mistake and failure is serious. I have trudged the Pennines at all hours and seasons and found them thrilling and perilous. The miles are long and the going wet and difficult. I must warn you that in these Pennines the snow may lie (and fall) from November to May and make the going heavy and route-finding terribly difficult.[2]

But if you're up for a challenge, read on…

To complement the main route the book will suggest circular walks, or linear ones assuming transport can be arranged, incorporating parts of the boundary, which is in fact how I did it. For simplicity I have described it in a general north-south-west direction although there is no reason why it can't be done the other way – again I did some sections that way. The total distance is about 45 map-miles and conveniently it falls onto just one

---

2 Palmer, William T., *Wanderings in the Pennines*, Skeffington & Son, 1951.

Ordnance Survey sheet – 1:25000 Explorer OL19, *Howgill Fells and Upper Eden Valley*. Inconveniently this is double-sided and the turn-over point will come when you are caught in a howling gale on Stainmore Summit while attempting to dodge the traffic on the A66 (don't even think of trying it)! It is a good idea to have the map to hand while reading the book as constant reference will be made to it and to save a lot of geographical explanation a degree of familiarity with the layout of the Pennines is assumed.

Also useful is the Cassini series of revised and updated versions of old OS maps published in the last ten years or so – if you can get hold of them. These correspond to the modern Landranger series, Sheets 91 and 98 covering the route except for the western edge of the Howgills. There are three editions, 1852-66, 1903-04 and 1924-25. They provide a fascinating insight into how the area has changed and also how OS mapping itself has developed. The drawback is that they are no longer generally available in pre-printed form but I believe it is possible to create personalised copies through the Cassini website.[3] Also the National Library of Scotland has most of the historical maps available for viewing online[4] but this in no way equates to actually spreading the physical map out on a table and poring over it. Put the three editions side-by-side and compare them – it's better than squinting at a computer screen where you can't get a complete overview. The internet is all very well and useful but it often pays to do things the traditional way – it may seem old-fashioned to some people but it's far more satisfying! More on this, and on the Ordnance Survey, later.

How long will the walk take? Palmer doesn't say. He mentions only one overnight camping stop but to do the whole route in two days is a tall order. However, as will be shown shortly, doing so was well within Palmer's capabilities. Today maybe the SAS or Royal Marines could do it but this book is for lesser mortals and anyway, why hurry?

I've broken the route down into sections for ease of description but these can be varied depending on the individual, bearing in mind the necessity of travelling to a starting point and, perhaps more importantly, getting home again. If attempting it as an expedition over a number of consecutive days remember that there are hardly any accommodation options, the only alternatives being wild-camping (technically illegal without the landowner's permission) or going off-route to find lodgings or a suitable camp site. That

---

3 cassinimaps.co.uk
4 nls.uk

INTRODUCTION

said, apart from the Warcop Training Area where some restrictions apply, it is all Open Access land and can be freely walked over. A word of warning here; the boundary crosses many areas which are environmentally sensitive. You are advised not to follow the trackless stretches (Maize Beck to Nine Standards Rigg) during the critical time for ground-nesting birds (May to July) and these should not be undertaken *at any time* by groups of more than three or four persons. This is ground which must be trodden lightly. But, as I've told you, it's God's Own County – however you choose to do it, enjoy it!

If you've read this far and are eager to get going that's great; but first we must say something about the boundary itself and about the man whose idea it was to walk it – William T. Palmer, FRGS, MBOU, FSA(Scot.).

William Thomas Palmer, 1877-1954

So who was William Thomas Palmer? Over the many years I had possessed his *Odd Corners in the Yorkshire Dales* I had been curious about the letters which appeared after his name on the title page – FRGS, FBOU, FSA (Scot). The second and third groups were at that time unfamiliar to me but FRGS – one doesn't get to be a Fellow of the Royal Geographical Society by simply picking up an atlas and going on a few foreign holidays. This must be a man of some note. I later acquired two or three more of his books, which showed that he was born in Westmorland and knew the Lake District intimately; that he had at least one daughter; that he had spent many years exploring not only the Lakes but also the Pennines, Scotland, Wales and even the South of England; that he must have been a fairly prolific writer over a period of some decades and that, at the time of his walk along Yorkshire's Wildest Boundary, around 1936, he must have been in middle age.

My interest at that time didn't extend to any more than curiosity but when I decided to follow in his footsteps I thought I should do a bit of research. Initial investigations produced almost nothing except that some of his books were available second hand on websites. How could it be that someone like him seemed to have disappeared from the radar? Then I chanced upon a press report to the effect that a lady from Workington, Sheila Richardson, had delivered a lecture about him to a Cumbrian local history society and had published a biography of him, called *The Forgotten Man of Lakeland*.[1] The report was of course quite brief but it gave me enough information to work on.

I found the biography in Kendal Library and later obtained my own copy – and there it was, the full story of his life and career, meticulously researched and recorded in detail. The first few pages indicated that Mrs. Richardson had run up against the same problem as I had – his books could be found in libraries or second hand bookshops but there was nothing about the man himself. By persistent investigation she traced his only

---

[1] Richardson, Sheila, *The Forgotten Man of Lakeland*, Mill Field Publications, 1997.

granddaughter and more distant relatives plus people who knew him or knew of him and gradually pieced together a picture of someone who proved to be quite a remarkable man, someone who had indeed been unjustly forgotten.

I subsequently contacted and corresponded with Mrs. Richardson; I have no wish to captialise on her hard work by slavishly reiterating any substantial parts of her book – you must read it for yourself – so in the following account I will relate only the basic facts of the life of William Thomas Palmer, *The Forgotten Man of Lakeland*.

He was born on the 8 July 1877, in Bowston, near Kendal, the fourth of five children of James and Jane Palmer who both had their roots fixed deeply in the Westmorland countryside. Like many rural families in the late nineteenth century the Palmers were far from wealthy and lived on a 'make do and mend' basis, with scant resources. William's education too was typical of the times and can probably be described as little more than basic. He did, however, receive a good grounding in history and geography and he developed a great appetite for reading, all of which were to stand him in good stead in his later professional life.

During his childhood and schooldays William was continually in contact with country people and country life, learning much about nature, farming, shepherding and countryside traditions and practices and became what would now be called a true outdoor type.

On leaving school William took the usual path into the world of work by becoming a farm hand. His job as a shepherd took him far into the Lakeland fells in all weathers and the practical knowledge he gained, together with his earlier learning, shaped his future when he changed direction and started work in the printing shed of a Kendal newspaper. His contact with the fast-moving media environment, to use another modern term, was very different from his previous experience but it excited and inspired him and, becoming a junior reporter, he took his first steps on the road to a career as a professional writer and journalist. The words 'took his first steps on the road' are highly appropriate considering the activities which formed the subject matter of the greater part of his writing.

In 1901 William married Annie Ion, a member of a well-connected and respected Kendal family. She was a gifted lady of considerable intellect who shared many of William's interests and supported him in his work throughout their long and happy marriage. The dedication in *Wanderings in the Pennines* is 'To my Wife, the Lady at my Elbow, who camped and explored the Pennines with me'.[2] Their talents were passed on to their two daughters, Annie and Jean, who both embarked on their own successful careers.

In the late nineteenth century travel was still the preserve of the well-to-do. Motor vehicles were as yet almost unknown, journeys by horse or by coach were scarce and expensive and there were isolated places where even in the age of railway mania the steam engine had failed to penetrate. The only way for people of limited means to get about, if they had the inclination to do so, was to walk. William had that inclination a-plenty and walk he most certainly did. From his teenage years he regularly set off before dawn, or in the middle of the night, simply to get to the start of a walk and would be out for a full 24 hours or even more, covering mileages which would put modern so-called long distance walkers to shame. His first such walk, in 1894, aged seventeen, was 85 miles.

His covering of Yorkshire's wildest boundary in two days would have been far from extraordinary although he does admit that he found parts of it hard going. His account in *Wanderings in the Pennines* of a winter crossing of Mickle Fell, in conditions which would have made me think twice about setting foot outside the door, proves he was a tough nut, so if he says it's hard, then it's hard.[2] The stories of his expeditions suggest that some bordered on the foolhardy or even downright dangerous.

He was not alone in accomplishing such feats. The late sixteenth and early seventeenth centuries produced Thomas Coryate of Odcombe in Somerset, who published very popular accounts of his travels on foot through Europe before succumbing to drink and dysentery while on his way to India, and John Taylor of Gloucester, the 'Water Poet', who served in the Navy and as a Thames waterman and drew attention to himself by a series of eccentric journeys including rowing a paper boat from London to the Isle of Sheppey with oars made from fish tied to canes, and walking to Scotland without carrying any money.[3]

Nearer to Palmer's own time, his fellow Westmerian the poet William Wordsworth and the Whitby lawyer and banker George Weatherill, who gained fame as a watercolour artist, were also noted for their long journeys on foot. William's inspiration came from George Borrow of *Wild Wales*

---

2 Palmer, William T., *op. cit.*, 1951.
3 Hillaby, John, *Journey through Britain*, Constable & Co., 1968.

WILLIAM THOMAS PALMER

William Palmer as a young man, image with thanks to Sheila Richardson.

fame and Canon A. N. Cooper of Filey whose walking exploits took him all over Europe.

In 1918 the Palmers moved to Liverpool which afforded more opportunities for William's career advancement as a journalist. This meant the mountains of North Wales and the hills of the Peak District and the Pennines were within relatively easy reach and he took full advantage of them. There were also frequent visits to Scotland and wherever he went he did so regardless of season or weather. Through all these journeys his store of knowledge and experience increased and was carefully recorded, to be used in his writing as and when the appropriate occasion arose.

William Palmer wrote more than thirty books between 1902 and 1952 and while they were at times produced somewhat erratically many ran to several editions, proving their popularity. He wrote from both head and heart; head because he wrote from personal experience, heart because he loved and understood the subjects he wrote about. Even after so many years his words remain relevant; his books are still eminently readable, being written in an easy uncomplicated style with none of the wordy pomposity found in many writers of the late nineteenth and early twentieth centuries. He stimulates interest and curiosity. It is fascinating to compare his descriptions and impressions of places and features with how they appear to us today and to link the historical events he mentions with what we may already know from other sources. It was exactly these motivations that caused me to undertake the boundary walk, to compare my experiences with his and to see what has changed, how it has changed and, probably most importantly, why it has changed. I hope that at least some of this will become clear in the following chapters.

In this brief overview of William Palmer's life I have concentrated on the aspects most relevant to this book – his roots, his formal and informal education, his experience as a walker and his competence as a writer. Much more, including his exploits as an accomplished rock-climber (he was an original member of the Fell and Rock-Climbing Club and for several years the editor of its journal), and his enthusiasm for camping, cycling and country sports, can be found in Sheila Richardson's biography, together with the story of his sad decline in health due to the onset of the debilitating illness now known as Huntington's Disease which led to his death in 1954. An hereditary condition, it subsequently claimed the lives of both his daughters.[4]

---

4 Richardson, Sheila., *op. cit.*, 1997.

WILLIAM THOMAS PALMER

All in all, William Palmer comes over as a determined and perservering individual, with a set and clear-sighted purpose in life and the knowledge and capacity to achieve it, and yet remaining a relatively modest man, never boasting about his many accomplishments; and what of those letters after his name? FBOU is Fellow of the British Ornithological Union, while FSA (Scot) is Fellow of the Scottish Society of Antiquaries. As for FRGS it turns out that William did in fact achieve the position by simply filling in the proposal form and paying the subscription! It must have been easier in those days. However, I have read the current form of application for election to the Fellowship and it seems to me that he would have been well entitled to the honour on the strength of his publications alone and the Society would probably have welcomed him with open arms. He deserves to be remembered.

So why is William Palmer not remembered today? It may well be due in part to his self-effacing nature; but as Sheila Richardson points out, in his day there was no mass media, mass communication or mass advertising; by and large there wasn't even mass travel in the way we would know it today. By the time these came about William Palmer was long departed and his works had been eclipsed by those of Alfred Wainwright. But William knew the Lakeland fells inside out long before Wainwright began even thinking about them. If this book does just a little to redress the balance it will have been worth the effort made in researching and writing it. To emphasise the point, and I speak as one who has walked thousands of miles in Britain and on four of the seven continents, William Palmer inspired me to walk the boundary; while I appreciate Wainwright's skill as an author and artist, as a walker he has never inspired me in any way.

Yorkshire as a County

Borders and boundaries are everywhere; from a sulky teenager's barricaded bedroom door to international frontiers with checkpoints, officials and guards, they affect us all in some way and have always been a red-hot political topic. They are well-known in the animal kingdom too; the robin, recently elected Britain's National Bird, is noted for being fiercely, even viciously, territorial; the neighbourhood tom cat may be heard loudly proclaiming lordship over his domain on his nightly patrols (get him neutered!); the sheep roaming the uplands which feature so prominently in this book have their own 'heafs' and seldom stray beyond them.

Some boundaries of our own creation are visible, others are not. The Yorkshire boundary has bits of both. I've already mentioned the fences and watercourses; there are boundary stones too, as will be seen later. But as will also be shown, there are stretches where there is no clear evidence of the county's limits.

So how, when and why did Yorkshire come into being? It's a long and complex story and only the bare bones can be given here. There is no precise date of its origin as a county; it is first mentioned as 'Yorkshire' (Old English *Eoforwicscire*)[1] in a writ of Edward the Confessor dating from between 1060 and 1065 but as an entity its existence goes much further back and may have corresponded to the old Anglo-Saxon kingdom of Deira.[2] By 651 AD this had unified with the northern kingdom of Bernicia to form a single kingdom north of the Humber (North-Humbria or North-Humber-Land).[1] The old kingdom of Deira was conquered and settled by Viking invaders following the capture of York in 867 AD so Northumbria appears to have divided again, basically along the course of the River Tees[1] (Scandinavian place-names are common in Teesdale but less so in Weardale, only a few miles further north, where 'becks' become 'burns').[3] The resulting Viking kingdom of York survived until the death of the last Viking king,

---

1 Townend, Matthew: *Viking Age Yorkshire,* Blackthorn Press, 2014.
2 Hey, David: *A History of Yorkshire: County of the Broad Acres*, Carnegie, 2005, 2011.
3 Earnshaw, Alan: *The Wear Valley Way, Discovery Guides*, Local History Series, 1983.

YORKSHIRE AS A COUNTY

Erik Bloodaxe in 954AD and the old county of Yorkshire can generally be defined as corresponding with this kingdom. It is the only northern county created before the Norman Conquest and the only one to appear in the Domesday Book of 1086.

Christopher Saxton, appropriately as far as this book is concerned, was a Yorkshireman, born around 1542 at Dunningley, south of Leeds. His death is not recorded but we know he was still alive in 1608. His chosen profession as a surveyor was fortuitous, for from the mid-sixteenth century onwards there was a major redistribution of land resulting from the Dissolution of the Monasteries and the new class of landed gentry required the services of experienced surveyors to map their holdings accurately. British county cartography originated with Saxton's county survey, published as an atlas of England and Wales in 1579. Considering the basic surveying methods and equipment available at the time his maps are notable for their high standard of technical execution and their remarkable precision. They provided the foundation for future cartographers well into the eighteenth century.[4] His 1577 map of Yorkshire clearly delineates the Ridings; although his representation of upland areas is somewhat pictorial, rivers, villages, etc. are shown accurately and demonstrate that broadly speaking the boundary was the one that existed until 1974.

'Broadly speaking' is right, but has the boundary remained unchanged in its detail? Not by any means. David Hey, in *A History of Yorkshire*, says that the southern boundary with Nottinghamshire was realigned in Norman times and significantly for our particular focus the north-western boundary may also have been amended at the same time. Unfortunately he doesn't elaborate but Westmorland, along with the other northern counties, was created in the twelfth century so perhaps its establishment included such an 'amendment'.

From Anglo-Saxon times, through the Middle Ages and beyond, kings made grants of land to those among the nobility who had served them well (and conversely confiscated them again when relations turned sour); similarly with the monasteries. They in turn made grants to those lower down the hierarchy, so through the ages favoured families and institutions came to own vast swathes of the country. In addition, during the same period England was divided into a bewildering array of administrative and

---

[4] Rawnsley, John E.: *Antique Maps of Yorkshire and Their Makers*, MTD Rigg Publications, 3rd edition, 1983.

ecclesiastical areas – hundreds, wapentakes, manors, liberties, sokes, townships, parishes, to list but a few.[5] It is neither necessary nor desirable to describe them here; what is important is that they all had boundaries and those boundaries had to be defined, so how was it achieved?

Dr. Stephen Walker, in his thoroughly researched book *Nine Standards: Ancient Cairns or Modern Folly?* presents compelling arguments for the possibly prehistoric origins of the nine large hilltop structures which overlook Kirkby Stephen and the Eden Valley.[6] His conclusions, moreover, are based on investigations emanating from a wide variety of starting points; these have unearthed a great deal of information about boundaries and as the Nine Standards are very close to the route of our walk this information is directly relevant.

The grants of land referred to above were made when the wild uplands of northern England were a frontier zone and boundaries were seldom marked on the ground or laid down in law. At the time of the Domesday Book, Cumbria was part of Scotland. There was much dispute over grazing rights, common lands and mineral and mining rights, leading to a great deal of litigation, some of which dragged on for years.[7] Such a case will be examined later.

Not every dispute ended up in court – they were sometimes contested in other ways. Palmer has this to say:

> this ridge of the Pennines runs on in a long continuity through different counties, and the boundaries of manors and townships are none too distinct. Occasionally the shepherds pass a few high words about their grievances, but never to the ancient extent.

This hints perhaps that violence may have been used in former times. He then includes a long quotation, which I've abbreviated, but doesn't say where it comes from:

> Even shepherds are sometimes as jealous of encroachments on their ancient sheep feedings as monarchs are about the boundaries of their dominions. In one of these pastoral brawls one of the contestants, with his back against

---

5 Parker, Mike: *Map Addict: A Tale of Obsession, Fudge and the Ordnance Survey*, Collins, 2009.
6 Walker, Stephen: *Nine Standards: Ancient Cairns or Modern Folly?* Hayloft Publishing, 2008.
7 Raistrick, Arthur: *The Lead Industry of Wensleydale and Swaledale: Vol 1 – The Mines*, Moorland Publishing Co., 1975.

a rock, commences the attack with a loud volley of opprobrious epithets, while his antagonist, from a trembling peatmoss, repels the onset with personal implications and family allusions... Having exhausted their ammunition, they separate, each striking homeward with an air of triumph and defiance.[8]

In an age of general illiteracy when no accurate maps existed some means had to be found of establishing boundaries and this was often done by 'perambulations', the walking or riding of the boundaries by the landowners, or more likely their agents and tenants on either side, establishing marker points and fixing the lines between them. There is evidence that these took place at least as far back as the fourteenth century and maybe even earlier and continued well into the nineteenth century.[6] Where written records of these perambulations exist they invariably follow a certain formula: they list the names of those present and their official positions; they list significant landmarks and landscape features and though the spelling and even the place names may have changed the routes are often traceable on modern maps. The descriptions ramble on without punctuation or pauses and have something of the character of recitations, perhaps so they could be more easily committed to memory at a time when the bulk of the population was illiterate.[6] Throughout, the curious phrase 'as Heaven's water deals', or similar, occurs frequently, signifying that in the uplands boundaries often followed the watershed between river catchment areas – this was not always as obvious as it might appear.

Among the papers in the Hanby Holmes collection in Durham County Record Office, relating to a dispute which will be described more fully later, there is a copy of the *Mid-Cumberland & North Westmorland Herald* of 19 September 1896, carrying an interesting and amusing account of one of these perambulations around Hartley, near Kirkby Stephen. This seems to suggest that in later times at least these affairs were undertaken as a matter of tradition regardless of the particular rights and wrongs of the situation and afforded an opportunity for a good old-fashioned booze-up. Sub-titled 'A Day Among the Peat Haggs', it contains phrases, quoted here by permission of Durham County Record Office,[9] which conjure up images familiar to anyone who has walked the Pennine hills in the frequently inclement weather: '...high wind blowing... arduous task of breasting the

---

8 Palmer, William T., *op cit*, 1951.
9 Durham County Record Office, D/HH6/6/1-70

hills... unable [because of the conditions] to take the names of all present... gale of wind, hats tied down... large crowd scrambling, jumping and tumbling among the peat haggs...'

There are protests and disputes along the way which appear to be almost scripted: 'You are entirely in the wrong and we are entirely in the right,' says Mr. Shepherd for Sir Richard Musgrave of Hartley.

'It is always the way on these occasions' replies Mr. Hudson for Captain Lyell of Muker.

The day is rounded off with 'refreshments' (the report doesn't elaborate) and the staging of a number of wrestling bouts, very likely Cumberland wrestling, still a popular sport at agricultural shows, after which everyone returns home in a driving storm, a good time having been had by all.

The production of the first accurate Ordnance Survey maps made perambulations obsolete but that didn't stop them. They are often carried out today (we are doing it ourselves by following in Palmer's footsteps) but more often as social and community occasions rather than for any legal or administrative purpose. However, they are still regarded as events of local pride and tradition and despite the conviviality the Common Ridings of the Scottish Borders in particular are taken very seriously.

Accurate maps did not end the disputes either, as will be seen in the vicinity of Tan Hill; but these disputes, with all the wrangling, litigation and maybe even violence, and the consequent boundary alterations, were all relatively minor and localised and pale into insignificance when compared to the cataclysmic changes brought about by the Local Government Act 1972.

For on the 1st April 1974 – the date could not be more appropriate – when the Act came into force, Yorkshire, along with other counties, was butchered, bloodily and mercilessly, without any considerations of history, regional pride or traditions, or people's sense of identity, in the belief, widely held among officialdom and often shown to be mistaken, that bigger means better. Parts were incorporated into the new 'counties' of Humberside and Cleveland, the parts with which we are concerned were transferred to Cumbria (although remaining within the Yorkshire Dales National Park) and to County Durham and, most insulting of all, parts were handed to Lancashire and 'Greater Manchester' – this name alone demonstrates banal bureaucratic lack of vision. Had they no imagination?

The three Ridings which had lasted for a thousand years disappeared;

YORKSHIRE AS A COUNTY

the West Riding lost most of its territory to the new North Yorkshire and a hitherto unheard-of place called South Yorkshire, the shrunken remainder becoming West Yorkshire, and the East Riding ceased to exist, being absorbed, in my opinion, into the much-reviled Humberside. The changes caused a great deal of bitterness and resentment and still do.

This is nothing new. Sir Frank Stenton points out that the shire system in the tenth century was imposed by strong kings who were no respecters of either local traditions or ancient boundaries[10] – it was a case of the people having to like it or lump it (my words, not his). Simon Keynes says that the counties were created at different times and in different circumstances, with many taking their names from local centres of administrative or defensive importance,[11] that is, they were named after what became the county towns. These 'shires' often disregarded any pre-existing ethnic or cultural distinctions and illustrate the imposition on unwilling people of a system directed from the top down. The references actually relate to the Midland shires and while York-Shire obviously follows the naming trend, it is worth noting that its size, far exceeding that of any other county, and the coincidence of its boundaries with those of older kingdoms, suggest that despite their best efforts the kings were insufficiently powerful in the north to impose their will to the extent that they did further south.[12] That's Yorkshire stubbornness for you but unfortunately it wasn't enough to withstand the machinery of modern government.

As a sop to injured local pride the order invoking the creation of the new authorities stated that the old counties had not been abolished – the administrative areas had merely been re-arranged. With the old counties swiftly ceasing to be shown on all maps in everyday general use and the removal of the old boundary signs and the erection of new ones this was virtually meaningless and went unnoticed by the population at large.

However the spirit lives on – today the Yorkshire Ridings and Yorkshire Boundary Societies exist to preserve and promote the historic county of Yorkshire,[13] the 1st August is celebrated as Yorkshire Day from Dentdale to Holderness, from Saddleworth to Teesside, and the summit of Mickle

---

10 Stenton, Sir Frank: *Anglo-Saxon England*, Oxford University Press, 3rd edition, 1971.
11 Keynes, Simon: *Shires*, in Lapidge, Michael, Blair, John, Keynes, Simon & Scragg, Donald (Eds), *The Wiley Blackwell Encyclopaedia of Anglo-Saxon England*, 2nd edition, 2014
12 Falkus, Malcolm & Gillingham, John (Eds): *Historical Atlas of Britain*, Book Club Associates/Grisewood & Dempsey, 1981
13 yorkshireridings.org; yorkshireboundarysociety.wordpress.com

Fell, Yorkshire's highest hill but now allegedly in County Durham, is often decorated with White Rose flags. Some redress has been made in recent years – Humberside has been eliminated and the East Riding restored, the Borough of Redcar & Cleveland now announces on its signs that it is 'Part of the Historic North Riding of Yorkshire'[14] and since August 2016 more parts of Cumbria and, ironically, a small part of Lancashire have been included in the newly-extended Yorkshire Dales National Park. What goes around comes around...

The Government confirmed the old counties' position when on St. George's Day, 23 April 2013, the Rt. Hon. (now Sir) Eric Pickles, a Yorkshireman, then Secretary of State for Communities and Local Government, asserted that the traditional counties still exist and supported the Association of British Counties in promoting them. The Yorkshire Ridings and Boundary Societies continue to emphasise this assertion. While it may be factually and even legally so, from a practical point of view, with the old boundaries having been absent from commercial maps for over 40 years and with those people who have personal recollections of the old counties now at least in their mid-fifties, it is an assertion which will become increasingly difficult to sustain without a huge ongoing publicity campaign. As time goes on the attitude will perhaps be 'Who cares?' and that will be a great shame. The Boundary Society's Boundary Sign project, while laudable on the face of it, raises the question of confusion for those unaware of the county's past and present status, particularly visitors to the area. I have met people who have experienced just such confusion, as I will show later.

Yorkshire, of course, was not the only victim. The old rival Lancashire was dismembered while Westmorland suffered an even worse fate, being completely absorbed into Cumbria and disappearing from the map. William Palmer, always true to his Westmorland heritage, must have turned in his grave. Greatly affronted, the people of this proud, historic little county retaliated by re-naming their county town Appleby-in-Westmorland and proclaimed it on the signs at the edges of the town. For an amusing account of how the people of another, even smaller county, Rutland, fought to preserve their identity and for wry comments on boundaries in general read Mike Parker's book *Map Addict* (see note 5, page 26).

I was told recently by a resident of Kendal, who was old enough to re-

---

14 Regrettably not any longer – the signs have been replaced with 'seaside' ones – but at least they do say that Redcar & Cleveland is on the Yorkshire coast.

member and appreciate the fact, that prior to 1974 the Westmorland County Council finances were always in the black. Afterwards the thrifty ratepayers of rural Westmorland had to subsidise not only the urban and industrial areas of Carlisle and the Cumberland coast but also Barrow-in-Furness, newly acquired from Lancashire. So bigger means better, does it?

Throughout the rest of this book the new counties and their boundaries will be referred to only where the context requires it. Let me make it clear that I have no quarrel with Cumbria or County Durham as such – my grievance is with London-based bureaucrats who think they know better than anyone else – they suffer from tunnel-vision, they see only what they want to see and are blind to the fall-out which often results from the pursuit of their ideas and their obstinate determination to impose them on others.

Russell Grant is well-known as an astrologer; what may be less well-known is that he is a patron of the Association of British Counties. His book *The Real Counties of Britain* describes the post-1974 attempts by the civil service to establish and define the several different types of 'county', the resulting bureaucratic shambles and the spin put upon it in an effort to convince the public that it's what was wanted all along.[15] No wonder there is ignorance and confusion!

Studied dispassionately, perhaps some of the 1974 changes were logical; it's just that as a traditionalist I find them hard to stomach. Other changes, however, made no sense whatsoever; it is significant that the 'metropolitan counties' lasted a mere twelve years and that the whole set-up was re-vamped only ten years later. There have been other alterations since then, suggesting that it might have been better (and far less costly) to leave in place a system which had served adequately until then. I can speak with some experience as I was once a local government officer, working for a small district council which functioned relatively smoothly until it was absorbed by a larger authority, losing its identity in the process and attracting the usual opprobrium which continues to this day. I suppose that makes me a bureaucrat too, in a small way, but I got out before the changes took place.

Here I must digress for a while but with a purpose. I said that I have no quarrel with County Durham in itself and however one views the boundaries there is no doubt that for a small county it punches well above its weight. It has rich farmland, a Heritage Coast, history by the shed-load and some

---

15 Grant, Russell: *The Real Counties of Britain*, Virgin Publishing Ltd., 1996

of the grandest walking country anywhere. It has world-class attractions like the Bowes and Beamish Museums, the incomparable Durham Cathedral and the spectacularly successful Kynren open-air historical pageant in Bishop Auckland. And one must not forget the Angel of the North, the Sage Music Centre and the Baltic Centre for Contemporary Art in Gateshead and the National Glass Centre and Penshaw Monument in Sunderland; for just as surely as Mickle Fell belongs to Yorkshire these all belong to County Durham and not to 'Tyne and Wear' which, thankfully, is no more. (In fact it appears that this absurdly-named, functionless, pointless pseudo-county does still exist in law. That being the case, in the words of Mr Bumble in *Oliver Twist,* 'the law, Sir, is a ass, a idiot!' As a former lawyer I concur in his opinion).

I mention this for the simple reason that though Yorkshire to the core I've lived in County Durham quite contentedly for a number of years and I will defend it vigorously against anyone who tries to run it down – so there! And to prove it let's turn briefly to a subject dear to many a Yorkshireman's heart – cricket. The recent 'punishment' meted out to Durham County Cricket Club is despicable. Being upstart newcomers, by achieving so much in such a short time they have probably upset the old-school-tie brigade among cricket's top brass. Surrey or Middlesex or Kent would never have been treated so shabbily. Let's hope they recover quickly and belt 'em all over the park. Unfortunately they haven't made a good start.

I've ranted on at some length, maybe excessive length, but it is a subject about which I, like many others, have strong opinions; and although William Palmer gave me the idea of walking the boundary I also followed him to emphasise the continuing identity of Yorkshire, of Westmorland and indeed of County Durham as ancient and historic institutions which should not be allowed to fade from memory through officialdom's meddling. And now, having set the scene amid the landscape, the history and the politics, let's get down to the nitty-gritty – let's walk the North-West Frontier.

Cauldron Snout to Mickle Fell Summit

For the purposes of this book the 'North West Frontier' begins where the River Tees, plunging down the rocky defile of Cauldron Snout, is joined by Maize Beck. Here in the middle of the river the counties of Durham, Westmorland and the North Riding meet. There are two ways of getting there, both involving long approach walks which can take up most of a morning, at times crossing rough, rock-strewn ground, at the very edge of the water. They can be combined to form a circular walk (this means fording Maize Beck – see later). One leaves Langdon Beck or the nearby car park at Hanging Shaw, picks up the Pennine Way and follows the north bank of the Tees to its confluence with Maize Beck below Falcon Clints. The other route follows the south bank and is more remote and much less frequented. On

The start of the 'North West Frontier' – Maize Beck joins the River Tees below Cauldron Snout – Cow Green dam visible above – that dam' wall!

a fine spring morning both are delightful walks through solitude, with only the sound of the river and the calls of lapwing, curlew and plover and the drumming of snipe for company. Or is there something – or someone – else…?

Once upon a time, long, long ago, there lived in Teesdale a beautiful girl who was employed as a domestic servant in one of the 'mineshops', the lodging-houses provided for the lead miners whose work in these lonely hills meant they could not make the long journey between home and mine each day. There she met and fell in love with a handsome young miner and they spent many happy hours roaming the wild fells together. All went well until one day the young man told her that their romance was over – he was going away to seek his fortune in America. Distraught, she fled, running and running, coming at last to Cauldron Snout where, in despair, she threw herself to her death in the raging torrent.[1]

I first came to this atmospheric spot over twenty years ago, on a dry, still day in April, with a sky the colour of steel. Looking across to the waters' meeting it was possible to imagine a ghostly figure and perhaps to hear, mingling with the sound of the falls, the haunting voice of the Singing Lady of Cauldron Snout lamenting sadly for her lost love…

To bring one down to earth with a bump (maybe literally – I speak from experience) the scramble up the side of Cauldron Snout reveals the unwelcome sight of Cow Green Dam. The reservoir was built in the late 1960s after a long, acrimonious and ultimately unsuccessful political battle to prevent the flooding of an internationally important botanical site. A detailed, unbiased account of this battle, by Roy Gregory, can be found in Chapter 5 of *The Politics of Physical Resources*.[2] I never saw Cow Green before the reservoir was built so I can't comment on what may have been lost in landscape terms but it must have been an incredibly bleak and lonely location – nearby Meldon Hill, rising to the west, was cited recently by *Country Walking* magazine as the most remote summit in England – and maybe the stretch of water adds something to it; not so the dam itself.

Reservoirs constructed in Victorian times and into the early twentieth century were often built of stone and they have some architectural merit;

---

1 Parker, Malcolm & Tallentire, Lorne, *Teesdale and the High Pennines,* Discovery Guides, 1987.
2 Gregory, Roy, *The Cow Green Reservoir*, in Smith, Peter J. (Ed), *The Politics of Physical Resources*, Penguin Education/Open University Press, 1975.

Cow Green is Soviet Brutalist-style concrete and has no aesthetic value whatsoever. Probably those who approved and designed it thought that out here few people would see it – erroneous bureaucratic tunnel-vision again.

> *Now that river's not running as fast as it did,*
> *There's a dam there restricting the flow...*

The beautiful song *River Run*, by the Canadian songwriter James Keelaghan, was written about the Oldman River in Southern Alberta which was controversially dammed in 1991 but the words can well be applied to the upper Tees. They are reproduced here by kind permission of James himself.[3]

It is interesting to compare the fate of Upper Teesdale with that of another Yorkshire dale, Farndale in the North York Moors, where a similar reservoir scheme, at a similar time, was eventually rejected. The North York Moors had national park status, the North Pennines did not and it was not until 1988 that designation as an Area of Outstanding Natural Beauty was achieved. Would the Cow Green plan have gone ahead if the bureaucrats had not disregarded the North Pennines when national parks were first proposed?

The importance of Cow Green and its surroundings as a botanical site lies in its geology, combined with a sub-arctic climate. Much of the Pennine chain is composed of Carboniferous limestone laid down in a warm, shallow, tropical sea some 300-350 million years ago. Around 295 million years ago a vast sheet of igneous rock called dolerite was intruded into the country rocks to form what is known as the Whin Sill. 'Whin' and 'sill' are quarrymen's terms for a hard, dark-coloured rock and horizontal rock strata respectively. The Whin Sill outcrops in many places in North East England, on Holy Island and the Farne Islands, through southern Northumberland where Hadrian's Wall is built along its crags and most notably in Teesdale where great thicknesses of it form the dramatic cliffs of Holwick Scar, Cronkley Fell and Falcon Clints and the waterfalls of Cauldron Snout and High and Low Forces.[4]

This molten rock baked the surrounding limestone, crystallising it into a crumbly form known as sugar limestone, now the home of many rare

---

3 James Keelaghan© 1992, Tranquilla Music.
4 Forbes, Ian; Young, Brian; Crossley, Clive and Hehir, Lesley – *Lead Mining Landscapes of the North Pennines Area of Outstanding Natural Beauty*, Durham County Council, 2003

YORKSHIRE'S NORTH WEST FRONTIER

arctic-alpine plants, collectively called the Teesdale Assemblage, some of which are found nowhere else. In spring these fragile little jewels adorn the fells, the most exquisite being the blue or spring gentian and the mountain pansy. But don't expect to find the ground carpeted with them – they are there but they have to be looked for.

It is not only for its plant life that Teesdale is important; its bird life is also of international significance. In addition to the familiar upland species such as curlew, lapwing, plover, oystercatcher, wheatear (a handsome little bird and one of my favourites) and the ubiquitous red grouse, the endangered black grouse also has one of its remaining refuges here. In early spring these generally elusive birds gather at established sites to perform their courtship ritual, known as lekking. Go to a lek just before dawn in April, keep well away and use binoculars (don't get out of the car, it spooks the birds), listen and you will hear a curious chuckling and bubbling sound. As the light increases the male birds can be seen scuttling around like mechanical toys, tail feathers erect, wings outstretched but held low, heads down, jumping, posturing and sparring with each other. The females are harder to spot from a distance and if they are scared off by sudden movement the males will not display. The whole experience is rather surreal.

The Game and Wildlife Conservation Trust works with landowners, farmers and environmental groups to maintain and improve black grouse habitat and numbers. Because of their significance Cronkley Fell, Widdybank Fell and part of Mickle Fell form one half of the Moor House-Upper Teesdale National Nature Reserve, one of the most intensively scientifically studied sites in the world.

The Pennine Way has left the Yorkshire boundary and proceeds west, well away from Maize Beck, past the isolated Birkdale Farm and on to Moss Shop, maybe – who knows? – the place where the Singing Lady and her lover first met, but now no more than a huge tumbled pile of stones through which an ugly rubble estate track has been bulldozed. Another dreadful eyesore, this is hell to walk on. I had often wondered how the estate was permitted to cause such devastation, several miles of it, to what is not only a public right of way but also our principal National Trail until I was told by Andrew Morrow, the keeper at Birkdale, that the track had been put in because the old one was becoming washed out, exposing large stones.

Left: Lapwing and spring gentian from a painting by Judith Owston, Middleton-in-Teesdale.

I've since learned from another reliable source that although the work was done with official approval the problems stemmed from… no,' enough said; better leave it there.

Isolated Birkdale Farm – the Pennine Way runs past the house.

From Moss Shop a faint path heads down to Maize Beck and the boundary, entering the Warcop Training Area. On the other bank is the beginning of the fence which will be our guide all the way to Tan Hill and beyond.

Maize Beck is quite wide but unless there has been heavy rain it is not particularly deep and can be forded dry-shod if wearing gaiters; but the rocks are loose and slippery and a fall will result in a soaking and possible injury. If the water really is too deep the only alternative is to rejoin the Pennine Way and follow it upstream to the footbridge at Dobson Mere Foot then double back along the southern bank of Maize Beck. Swarth Beck still has to be crossed but this is a lesser obstacle. This adds some three or four miles to the walk and we haven't even started the climb up Mickle Fell!

Following the southern bank of Maize Beck from its junction with the Tees has the advantages of staying closer to the boundary and avoiding the

CAULDRON SNOUT TO MICKLE FELL SUMMIT

Mickle Fell from the north west – Maize Beck in the foreground.

beck crossing, although the way is rugged, with no discernible path. The view across to Cauldron Snout is spoiled by the sight of the dam above. The right of way ends at the water's edge opposite Birkdale Farm but the 1863 six inch Ordnance Survey map shows a ford here. According to Geoffrey N. Wright, in *Roads and Trackways of the Yorkshire Dales*, Birkdale was an important halt on a drove road from Scotland via Alston and South Tynedale, over Cronkley Fell by what is now known as the Green Trod, to Holwick and on to the eastern lowlands.[5] This may explain the anomaly as older maps show a path heading north-west from Birkdale over the shoulder of Meldon Hill towards Moor House where it joins the track to Tynehead and which may indicate the course of this drove road.

It is not shown on modern maps. I have attempted to trace it from both Birkdale and Moor House but the ground is criss-crossed by quad tracks here, there and everywhere and there is no evidence of anything identifiable as a more substantial or established track. It must have fallen out of use even before Palmer's time for coming from Garrigill on another of his Pen-

---

5 Wright, Geoffrey N., *Roads and Trackways of the Yorkshire Dales*, Moorland Publishing Co., 1985.

nine mega-walks he stayed at Moor House, then a working farm, where the lady told him that the track was 'little used and not easy to follow'. He continued to Cow Green on the opposite (Durham) bank of the Tees.[6]

Before the boundary fence is reached the route passes the ruins of Maize Beck Shop and enters the Warcop Training Area. This was established in 1942 and has been in continuous use ever since. The sound of gunfire can often be heard from the surrounding hills. Like many areas controlled by the military it is also scientifically important – its north-eastern section, including the northern slopes of Mickle Fell, overlaps part of the Nature Reserve – and the Ministry of Defence devotes considerable resources to promoting habitat conservation and improvement, demonstrating that the contrasting demands of military and wildlife are not mutually exclusive.

Numbered boundary stone by Maize Beck.

The boundaries of the Training Area are clearly shown on the Explorer map and there is no need to detail here the access arrangements; these are fully set out in a leaflet produced by the Ministry of Defence and on their website.[7] Suffice it to say that access to Mickle Fell, which is not owned by the Ministry of Defence, is by permit and there are only two official routes to the top, one from the north and one from the south. Our traverse of the fell ascends the former and descends the latter. Ministry of Defence

---

6 Palmer, William T., *op. cit.*, 1951.
7 www.access.mod.uk

staff at Warcop are very helpful in arranging permits but application needs to be made well in advance of any visit.

The fence begins right on the bank of Maize Beck and close by is the first of a series of numbered boundary stones which accompany it for many miles. Some have fallen over, some are half-buried, some are missing altogether, no doubt swallowed by the bog. The lettering suggests they date from the eighteenth century. Similar stones are found on other boundaries in the area.

Now the hard work starts. Palmer describes the fence and its path as being in excellent order. There is no path, just the fence climbing steadily, dead straight, up the hill and out of sight. He makes the ascent sound easy and quick but it isn't that simple. The slope is not excessively steep but the heather is long, the tussocks awkward and although there are worse bogs to come, numerous deep channels and pits make maintaining a straight line difficult. But at last the top is reached, close to the western edge of the ridge. The large, untidy summit cairn is a few hundred yards to the left across level, grassy ground and the first objective has been achieved!

Mickle Fell Summit to Ley Seat

Mickle Fell, at 2591 feet, is the highest hill in Yorkshire. Its name is derived from the Norse *mikhill* and *fjall*, meaning 'great hill'. Its isolation and access difficulties mean it is far less well-known and receives far fewer visitors than the celebrated Three Peaks of Whernside, Ingleborough and Pen y Ghent. It is a broad, curving, flat-topped ridge running west to east, about two miles long, with a steep slope at its western end and a gentler descent

Making a point on Mickle Fell summit.

towards the east. Its trig point is some distance east of the actual summit. In 1944 a Stirling bomber crashed on the fell killing all but one of the crew, one of a number of such accidents throughout the Pennines. The lone survivor, the rear gunner, Alan Small, with serious injuries including a broken leg, crawled to Birkdale Farm – the mind boggles! How determined people can be to survive when the chips are really down! Wreckage of the aircraft could be found many years later; the main parts were recovered in the 1970s[1] but I believe some remain although I haven't seen them.

On a clear day Mickle Fell boasts one of the finest viewpoints in the North Pennines, far better than Cross Fell, which is 339 feet higher and can be seen almost ten miles away to the north-west. To the south are the aforementioned Three Peaks and nearer, northwards, is Cow Green Reservoir with Cauldron Snout, just visible, foaming beneath it.

From the boundary fence the way down to Ley Seat presents a daunting prospect. Palmer describes the initial descent as having a 'tumbling appearance'. I'm not sure exactly what he means by that but the slope is steep, there are rocks scattered about and certainly a tumble here could have serious consequences. Lower down where the ground levels out it is riven with innumerable waterlogged channels between peat hags, forming islands in a seemingly interminable morass which has to be crossed. In his chapter on Teesdale Palmer says:

> ...the going is extremely wet, heavy and tiring. Peat hag, moss, bog, and marsh, with deep soft trenches ten feet deep, are met with every 20 yards... it's terrible country to cross.[2]

Progress is slow and keeping a straight line is impossible. Deviation from the fence is inevitable but it must be kept in sight, especially if visibility is poor, as it is easy to become disorientated, leading to futile wandering in a sodden peaty maze. The worst section is around Hanging Seal where the fence makes a pronounced turn to the left. Here it is joined by others for this is the meeting place of five parish boundaries – why here, of all places? Care must be taken to follow the correct fence onwards and to keep looking out for the boundary stones. The largest streams, Force Beck and Connypot Beck, have footbridges but there are plenty of others and the going doesn't get any easier until the range boundary is crossed at Hewits and the final

---

1 www.teesdalemercury.co.uk
2 Palmer, William T., *op. cit.* 1944.

descent ends on the B6276 Brough-Middleton road at Ley Seat.

Here is a post-1974 county boundary sign in the blue and gold of County Durham. A few years ago it read 'Welcome to County Durham, Land of the Prince Bishops'. Driving past one day I observed that 'County Durham' had been obliterated and 'Yorkshire' substituted in big white letters. I didn't do it; but while I deplore vandalism in general I couldn't help feeling an ever-so-slight touch of sneaking admiration for whoever did. The sign has since been replaced but it no longer says 'Welcome'.

Ley Seat is where the Ministry of Defence places its signs detailing the rules and regulations for access and flies a red flag when the range is operating. There are two small parking areas for this is where most people start their trek to the top. A few miles east is Grains o' th' Beck which deserves more than a passing mention and to which I shall return shortly. We are now in the first of two Lunedales encountered on this walk. (To avoid confusion the second, far to the south-west where our journey ends, will be referred to as the Lune Valley. It is in fact more correctly called Lunesdale or Lonsdale).

As we have already covered several miles over peaty country and have many more such miles to go, it may be as well to say something about this soggy brown stuff. Peat is partially decomposed vegetable matter, first formed in the wet, anaerobic conditions which developed after the last Ice Age. It is an early stage in a process of which the ultimate product is coal; that is many millions of years away, although we shall come across coal when we reach Tan Hill. Roots and other undecayed plant remains can frequently be found in exposed peat banks and are thousands of years old. Plants typical of upland peat bogs are sphagnum moss, cotton grass, crowberry, bog asphodel and cloudberry, known locally as knoutberry (knoutberry is often included in place-names, usually on high moorlands, throughout the northern Pennines).

Maintaining peat bogs is important because they act as sinks, absorbing and storing vast amounts of carbon dioxide; also, by soaking up huge quantities of rainfall and slowing surface run-off, they help to prevent flooding at lower levels. In view of the trend towards global warming, well-maintained peat bogs make a vital contribution to the environment.

After World War II, when Britain had been compelled to rely more and more on home-sourced food, the approach was to drain marginal lands in an attempt to make them more productive, so ditches known as grips were dug across the Pennine bogs. These can still be seen in many places, cutting across the hillsides in long, straight rows. The people responsible had little idea of what they were doing, they didn't appreciate the damage such a practice would cause and the experiment was doomed to failure. For peat, once dried out and eroded, becomes a carbon source. The carbon is released into the environment, the dry peaty dust is washed into watercourses causing them to silt up and the vegetation is destroyed and cannot recover, resulting in a vicious circle effect.

In recent decades the passage of thousands of walkers' boots has exacerbated the problem, particularly in the Peak District and parts of the South Pennines where great efforts have been made to restore the peatlands, with significant success. Visitor pressure in the North Pennines is less but there are still many badly eroded areas and the Area of Outstanding Natural Beauty Partnership has an ongoing programme of peat-depth surveying, grip-blocking and restoration work, in which I have taken part. So next time you curse as you put your foot in a particularly wet patch remember that, like the nasty medicine of your childhood, it's ultimately for your own

Inscription above doorway of the former school and chapel at Grains o' th'Beck

good. There will be more, *much* more about peat later on.

Grains o' th' Beck is now a single farm but like many Pennine settlements it was once considerably larger, even having its own school-cum-chapel and post office.[3] Both these buildings survive but no-one would guess their original function from their present appearance. The school/chapel is a stone building close to the farm entrance; it does have a lintel inscribed 'School & Chapel Erected by Subscription 1868' but few passers-by, especially motorists, would ever see it. The post office is a dilapidated black corrugated iron building on the roadside between the two bridges. The farm was once a pub; Palmer mentions it as being a refreshment house but no longer having a licence. In fact it closed as a pub in 1935. At the roadside opposite is a North Riding milestone indicating 'Brough 7 Middleton 7¼'. Sadly it is not in a good state and needs some tender loving care. The Milestone Society exists to record and restore old milestones and other roadside furniture. As a member I should like to see this one restored and if it were simply a matter of a new coat of paint I

North Riding milestone, Grains o' th' Beck.

---

[3] www.lunedale heritage.org.uk

would just do it and say nothing but it requires more than that. I must try the official route and approach Durham County Council. Put it on the to-do list...

Around the next bend in the direction of Middleton is a metal gate opening onto a broad estate track. This is not a right of way but the land it crosses is Open Access as far as the range boundary. It divides after about a mile and a half, one track heading right, leading to a tarn hidden in a hollow and known as Fish Lake. It is man-made, dating perhaps from the nineteenth century, and was stocked with fish for the sport of the local gentry and their guests. Behind it is the huge open scar of Close House Mine, worked for barytes as recently as the 1990s and designated a Site of Special Scientific Interest because of the presence of, among other minerals, an unusual example called rosasite.[3] Further up the valley is the secret waterfall of Arngill Force.

This is the gateway to an area of rolling hills and moors sometimes known as 't' Big Country'.[4] While it may not have the proportions of the Wild West it does stretch a long way, it is most certainly wild, and it takes some effort to explore properly. However, it is outside our present remit so we must return to the point where the track divides. The other branch heads down left, turns right, passes a couple of large barns, then after another mile or so reaches the Training Area warning signs. Here at a crossroads Open Access ends – a pity, as turning right presents a much easier route to Mickle Fell. At a time when I had applied for a permit I was following this track when I met one of the gamekeepers for Wemmergill Estate. Chatting to him, I mentioned the access arrangements. He gestured to the broad stony track running up into the hills.

'If you want to walk up that track,' he said, 'you're more than welcome.'
I thanked him. 'I wouldn't have gone without permission,' I said.
'No,' he replied, 'thank you for asking.'

The track climbs steadily, with a steepish section through High Crag, then becomes grassy as it reaches the end of the Mickle Fell ridge. From there it's an easy walk to the summit. Ascending from Ley Seat and returning via this track makes a good circular walk without having to cross the bogs twice – but do seek permission before going – you are there not by right but as a privilege so don't abuse it.

---

4 Brown, Iain, *The North Pennines: Landscape and Legend*, Summary House Publications, 2006.

Ley Seat to Stainmore Summit

Driving along the B6276 between Grains o' th' Beck and Thringarth one can see that Lunedale marks a significant change in the landscape. Instead of the rolling jumble of hills and secret valleys to the north the view south is one of a level plateau of almost uniform height stretching to the far horizon. Only the low isolated hill of Shacklesborough breaks the monotony. This is an area of broad flat ridges, all trending south-west to north-east, separated by shallow valleys, each with its own watercourse – Soulgill Beck, Rowantree Beck, Black Beck, Balder Beck becoming the River Balder (Balder comes from *Baldur,* a good old Norse name), Hunder Beck, Deepdale Beck, all with numerous smaller tributaries. This difference in scenery results from the Lunedale Fault, a major geological feature which runs west to east along the northern side of the dale. The downthrow is to the south, that is, the rocks on the southern side have been displaced downwards relative to those to the north.[1] This bleak and forbidding moorland declines gently southwards to cross the Stainmore Pass then rises again, with the River Greta, Sleightholme Beck, White Stone Gill and Frumming Beck continuing the sequence until the hilly country is reached again south of the Barras-Tan Hill road.

From Ley Seat the boundary fence, with its accompanying numbered stones, runs dead straight south-eastwards. Palmer's description of this stretch is not easy to reconcile with what appears on the map or with what is encountered on the ground. He suggests that the going is almost as bad as around Lune Head but to my mind it is much more straightforward than the boggy labyrinth on the southern slopes of Mickle Fell. He mentions a 'great mass of rock', presumably the cairn at Pind Hill, which may have been bigger in his day. Here the fence turns south and drops into the awkward little valley of Black Beck, then there is the broader, flat-bottomed trough of Balder Beck.

At the top of the bank on the other side is a bridlegate through which a

---

1 www.lunedale heritage.org.uk

bridleway, referred to by Palmer, comes up from Baldersdale towards North Stainmore. Following this makes a circular walk from Ley Seat, returning there via the B6276 and here I must relate a curious incident which happened when I was investigating this route, the strangest thing I've ever experienced in over fifty years of hill-walking and for which no-one seems able to offer an explanation.

Passing through the bridlegate I crossed a very wet, reed-choked valley bottom, reaching another gate from which a stony track led to a tarmac road and eventually to the B6276 as it climbs up from Brough. As I headed up the hill, coming slowly down towards me was a red lorry. It appeared to be a road mender's or roofer's lorry as it had a big square tank on the back, covered in tar drippings. It slowed as it approached.

'He's going to ask me something,' I thought. The lorry stopped and the driver leaned out, a round-faced man possibly in his forties, wearing gold-rimmed spectacles. He said something I couldn't catch. I motioned him to repeat it. Still I couldn't hear him.

I stepped into the middle of the road and peered up at him. He peered down at me. Then – 'Barcelona,' he said.

I must have looked puzzled. I *was* puzzled. Was it a statement? Was it a question?

'Barcelona,' he repeated. He had a definite foreign accent but the truck was right-hand-drive.

'You – from Barcelona?' I tried, pointing a finger.

'No! No! Barcelona! Citee!'

Could he really be asking the way to Barcelona, in the middle of the North Pennines? I have a little knowledge of Spanish but not nearly enough to carry on a conversation with someone three feet above me while standing in the middle of the road. I shrugged my shoulders and spread out my hands. He shook his head and drove slowly away.

The incident occupied my mind all the way back to Ley Seat. I have scoured the map for a farm or other settlement called Barcelona without success. In any case the man had definitely said 'citee'. The only suggestion I've been offered, by two friends, independently of each other, is that I was in a time warp. Maybe, but everything else about the day seemed real enough. Perhaps I really did see the Singing Lady back at Cauldron Snout…

Returning to the boundary, the Explorer map, while correct, is misleading. It shows the line of the bridleway from Baldersdale to North Stainmore as making a loop southwards up the slope from Balder Beck and through the bridlegate, which is the way I went. But in the bottom of the valley is a larger field gate which leads to a quad track, then to a longer section of stony track, thus avoiding the wet crossing of the valley and making it easier to get to North Stainmore.

The next section of the boundary to Stainmore Summit is rather like the curate's egg. There are parts which are level, relatively easy walking and others which are much rougher and boggier, with deep peat groughs, and there are several points to remark on. The fence is still accompanied by the numbered stones but a glance at the Explorer map shows that after about a mile of heading south-east it makes a 90 degree turn to the left. The grid reference of this point is NY874153 and although not named on the Explorer map the 1863 six inch map calls it Fox Yard. There follows a series of short, straight sections, reaching Beldoo Hill and forming a prominent north-east facing 'salient' feature. Palmer doesn't mention this specifically; he does mention hard going which becomes 'very bad' when the border turns sharp east but I found this the easiest bit. It may be that he followed a different line because the boundary here has been altered, although apparently before his time.

There is a reference in Iain Brown's *The North Pennines: Landscape and Legend* to an investigation by the Tithe Commissioners into a dispute about the exact line; unfortunately he quotes no source for this, nor even a date,[2] but the 1863 six inch map shows it running further to the south-west from Fox Yard to Deepdale Head. Also at Fox Yard the numbered boundary stones come to an end (the last one I noticed was No 6). There are stones along the present line but they are fewer, more roughly shaped and un-numbered. I have learned from several correspondents that the boundary between Brough and Bowes around here had been in dispute since the fourteenth century and that the arguments are very well documented in the Cumbria Record Office. It does not follow the watershed which in fact lies to the south-west over Great Knipe. I used this as my return route and will describe it shortly. The OS maps from 1895 onwards show the boundary as it stands at present, the dispute having finally been resolved in the late nineteenth century, an instance of the long-drawn-out nature of the arguments arising from the lack of clear definition.

Dropping down a slight incline to Rise Gill Foot I was surprised to find

---

2 Brown, Iain, *op. cit.*, 2006.

a shooting hut and a track heading east. Neither is shown on the 2016 Explorer map. There is a similar hut on the Pennine Way a few miles further east at the crossing of Deepdale Beck. This is not shown either and although both huts are quite new, the Deepdale one was certainly there in 2011 when I walked that part of the Pennine Way. Things change all the time, of course, and finding a hut that isn't shown on the map is a matter of only mild surprise and nothing to the one I got when I stepped inside.

Standing on the opposite side of the room, gazing out of the window, was a man, wearing an orange fluorescent waistcoat and, in complete contradiction, camouflage trousers. I had started out very early that day and finding him there at 9.30 on a Sunday morning, in the middle of nowhere, was enough to make my nerves jump. I expected him to turn round and was about to say 'Good morning' when I realised 'he' was a shop window mannequin which someone had carted up there for some unfathomable reason. At least he didn't ask me the way to Barcelona!

Pressing on, there are glimpses of the traffic on the A66 and soon it can be heard. It is fast-moving and incessant and trying to cross is simply not worth the risk. The only way to continue south is to arrange transport from here to Bowes and return to the lay-by on the opposite side. Alternatively a circular walk back to the North Stainmore area can be made by following the watershed north-west over Great Knipe to return to the Baldersdale bridleway. This is a strenuous route, harder I think than the boundary, with some deep peat groughs and awkward ground to cross, and oddly there are some more features which aren't shown on the map – a group of three smaller shooting huts and a track, a small quarry and a large ruined sheepfold. These huts are also relatively new but the quarry is much older, the sheepfold older still. All are significantly large enough to merit inclusion on a map scale of 1:25000 yet none of them features on the most recent edition. Strange.

At nearby North Stainmore is the Punch Bowl Inn, abandoned after it was bypassed when the A66 was improved in the 1990s and now a sad sight. It is said to be haunted by the ghost of a man murdered there after an argument over stolen treasure which is supposedly buried in the grounds. Seeing it in its present state one can well believe it. There are also tales of association with Dick Turpin.[3]

---

3 Robertson, Dawn, with photographs by Koronka, Peter, *Secrets and Legends of Old Westmorland*, Pagan Press and Cumbria Library Service, 1992.

YORKSHIRE'S NORTH WEST FRONTIER

I admit I didn't find this section of the walk particularly enjoyable. I think it's the flat, featureless aspect of the landscape, despite the good view northwards back across Lunedale. Although I love the North Pennines they often seem to have a slightly hostile, intimidating atmosphere, giving the feeling that anything might happen. I very rarely experience this in the North York Moors, which I've explored for the last fifty-plus years. It's the result, I think, of the lonely isolation and bleakness of the Pennines combined with the generally hard going; but that, without any doubt, is part of the attraction.

Stainmore Summit to Tan Hill

The area commonly known as Stainmore, perhaps originally Athelstane's Moore, is a vast shallow depression which crosses the Pennines at what is their widest but also one of their lowest points. It has thus been an important east-west route since prehistoric times. The Romans, recognising its strategic location, transformed the ancient way into a major military highway with forts at each end at Bowes and Brough, one at Maiden Castle near the Summit and a series of camps and signal stations in between. According to Andrew Bibby in his book *The Backbone of England*, which describes his journey following the Pennine watershed from the Peak District to Tynedale, there has been some debate in recent years about the exact nature of the Romans' presence here[1] but I'm in no way qualified to comment. In fact I often find the Romans rather boring. They were just too damn good at everything. Be that as it may, Stainmore has remained a significant transport artery ever since, used by Viking invaders, Scottish stock raiders, packhorse merchants, cattle drovers, stagecoaches, steam trains, military convoys and an ever-increasing volume of modern-day traffic. Even so it is still at the mercy of the elements; in winter and occasionally at other times it is often one of the first routes to be closed by high winds or blizzards.

A short distance east of the summit stands a stone column, all that remains of Rey Cross. Edmund Bogg (what a brilliant name for someone writing about the Pennines!) in *The Wild Borderland of Richmondshire*, written at the end of the nineteenth century, calls it Roi or Rere Cross, the 'Cross of Kings', the kings being those of England and Scotland who met here to define their respective domains in the tenth century.[2] This suggests that the name derives from the French *roi* but the suggestion is questionable in view of the fact that it was erected more than a century before the Norman Conquest. It is more likely that it comes from the Norse word *hreyr*,

---

1 Bibby, Andrew, *The Backbone of England: Landscape and Life on the Pennine Watershed*, Frances Lincoln, 2008.
2 Bogg, Edmund, *The Wild Borderland of Richmondshire: Between Tees and Yore*, Popular Edition, 1909.

Rey Cross, Stainmore.

meaning a boundary stone. However, the cross is associated with another king whom I have mentioned before.

Erik Bloodaxe – the very name conjures up visions of rampaging Viking raiders leaping ashore from their longships but in fact the last Viking king of York appears to have been a somewhat unassuming fellow. There is some disagreement between authorities; he may have had two reigns and even his identity has been questioned,[3] but it seems that he was killed in 954AD, not in a full-scale battle but in an ambush. Erik was accompanied at the time by a number of high-ranking chieftains from Orkney and the Hebrides and their deaths so far from York, in 'a certain lonely place called Steinmor', suggests that they were caught while fleeing towards Scotland.[3] It is said that history is always written by the victors but in Erik's case the records indicate sympathy, saying that he was 'betrayed' and 'treacherously killed'. Whatever the circumstances, legend had it that Rey Cross was erected on the site of the murders so when improvements were carried out to the A66 in the 1990s, which necessitated the relocation of the cross, excavations were undertaken and nothing was found. Today Rey Cross stands alongside the eastbound carriageway of the A66, complete with its own small layby and information board. I'm sure Erik would be pleased he isn't forgotten.

Strangely, although both Edmund Bogg and William Palmer mention Rey Cross, neither makes any reference to Erik; in fact Palmer, in his *Odd Corners* chapter on Teesdale, says that the cross marked the grave of the Pictish King Rodric who was killed in 73AD by Marius, after whom West-mare-land is named. He quotes the twelfth century chronicler Geoffrey of Monmouth as his source but William Rollinson says the name Westmorland actually comes from the Anglian Westmaringaland, meaning 'land of the western border',[4] while Kenneth Cameron's *English Place Names* gives it as the 'land of the Westmoringas',[5] the 'people who live west of the Moor'. Perhaps Palmer revised his opinion later as he does mention Erik in *Wanderings in the Pennines*.

During the Middle Ages rest houses for travellers in this wild and dangerous place were established, probably by monks. These were known as *spitals* (an abbreviation of hospital whose original meaning is guest house)

---

3 Townend, Matthew, *op. cit.*, 2014.
4 Rollinson, William, *A History of Cumberland and Westmorland,* Phillimore & Co., 1978.
5 Cameron, Kenneth, *English Place Names,* Batsford, 1996.

and the name survives in several locations on Stainmore. There are Spital High Cottages, Spital Grange, Spital Park, Spital Hill and Old Spital and one of them, suggested by Bogg and Palmer, was previously the Old Spital Inn, which was the setting for the tale of the Hand of Glory.[6]

The Hand of Glory was a charm, the hand of a hanged and gibbeted man, preserved by a revolting process, fitted with a candle made from the same unfortunate man's fat, which when lit and passed in front of a sleeping person made it impossible to rouse that person. There is a specimen of this type of grisly relic in Whitby Museum, believed to be the only one still in existence.

Towards the end of the eighteenth century an old woman called at the Old Spital and asked to stay the night but as she had to depart very early she would sleep in the kitchen if breakfast could be left ready for her. This was done and the family went to bed; but a serving-maid, suspicious of the stranger, herself lay down in the kitchen and pretended to sleep. Sure enough, she realised the old woman was really a man who, believing the girl to be asleep, produced the Hand of Glory, lit the candle, passed it in front of the girl's face and said: 'Let those who sleep be asleep; let those who are awake be awake.' Going to the door he whistled for his companions but the girl jumped up, pushed him outside, locked the door and ran to wake the family. She could not rouse them until she remembered to throw a bowl of milk over the candle (water was no use) whereupon the son of the house fired at the would-be robbers and in the morning bloodstains were traced for some distance. According to Bogg the girl's daughter was still alive in the 1860s and often related the story. At the time the inn was owned by one George Alderson. Alderson is a common surname in the Dales, especially in Swaledale and Wensleydale and on Stainmore, and George's descendants still live in the area. The Hand of Glory remained in the family's possession for many years.

The 'North West Frontier' crosses two railways, one very much alive and kicking, the other long since dead and largely forgotten, at least by the majority, but both with epic stories to tell. Heading south from Stainmore Summit the boundary crosses a couple of hundred yards or so of very long grass and reeds then drops down a steep-sided cutting to land on the trackbed of the former Stainmore Railway.

In 1857 the South Durham & Lancashire Union Railway began con-

---

6 Robertson, Dawn, and Koronka, Peter, *op. cit.*, 1992.

Track bed of the former Stainmore Railway near Ay Gill.

struction of a line to link the East Coast main line at Darlington with the West Coast main line at Penrith via the Eden Valley and at Tebay via the Lune Valley, initially to carry coal and coke from the Durham coalfields to the ironworks on the west coast and bring back good quality ironstone from the west to mix with the Cleveland ores used on Teesside. Once the highest main line in England it opened for freight in July 1861 and for passengers in August of the same year, some fifteen years before the more famous Settle to Carlisle line. The engineer was Thomas Bouch and the completion of the line was a triumph for him, carried through against all the odds of difficult terrain, constant bad weather and many constructional hurdles.[7]

Barras (originally Barhouse, signifying the presence of a toll-bar) was the highest main line station in England until Dent opened in 1877. Now a private house, it offers its occupants a superb view of the Eden Valley stretching far out towards the Solway Firth, with the ramparts of the East Fellside to the right, the Howgills and Mallerstang to the left and the Lakeland fells in the distance. The massive cast iron girder structure of Belah

---

7 Walton, Peter, *The Stainmore and Eden Valley Railways,* Oxford Publishing Co., 1992.

Viaduct, sadly dismantled after closure, was an engineering masterpiece. Unfortunately for Bouch it was another girder construction which ruined his career when the Tay Bridge collapsed while a train was passing over it, causing a number of fatalities.[8]

Inevitably the line had its operating difficulties, often being blocked by snow for long periods, and conditions for the railwaymen, working in appalling weather in those high, windswept, snowbound places, were brutal. Declining usage led to closure procedures beginning in 1952; all the usual deceitful bureaucratic dirty tricks were employed – manipulating passenger numbers and income figures by taking counts at periods of least usage, artificially inflating maintenance expenditure ('if they paint your station they must be going to close it') and holding 'public consultations' at times and in places which those most likely to object to closure found impossible to reach. The line finally closed in 1962 and was dismantled with almost obscene haste soon afterwards to forestall any sort of preservation movement. As a final indignity part of the trackbed west of the summit was buried

Replica sign on Stainmore Summit – the original was removed to the National Railway Museum in York.

beneath the A66 road improvements.[8, 9] Now the dedicated volunteers of the Stainmore Railway Company at Kirkby Stephen and the Eden Valley Railway at Warcop keep vestiges of the line operating, while parts around Winton, Hartley, Kirkby Stephen, Stenkrith and Smardale have been turned into pleasant walkways. In addition, the section from near Barras Station House to Stainmore Summit is held in trust by the Stainmore Railway Company with the legal obligation to use it solely for the public good, i.e. as a footpath or indeed as part of a revived railway. The ultimate aim of the volunteers is to reinstate the entire line; I wish them luck but I fear I shall be pushing up the daisies long before it happens.

The next section of the boundary can be incorporated into a long but exhilarating walk starting at Tan Hill or Sleightholme Farm, south-west of Bowes, and following the Pennine Way towards the River Greta which, though often dry owing to its porous limestone bed, is crossed by the natural slab of limestone known as God's Bridge. Up the rise the Pennine Way

The former Barras Station House (previously an hotel) overlooking the Eden Valley.

---

8 Walton, Peter, *op. cit.*, 1992.
9 Williams, Michael, *The Trains Now Departed,* Preface Publishing, 2015.

meets the old railway and it would be good to follow it all the way to Stainmore Summit. Unfortunately it is all private land as far as Old Spital and, at the time of writing, after a couple of hundred yards the track is blocked by a wire mesh fence at least eight feet high and which if I remember correctly is electrified.

Instead of dropping down to God's Bridge it is necessary to leave the Pennine Way where it passes through a gate and follow the wall marking the edge of the Open Access land. Heading west for some four miles, two areas of rough grassland are crossed, separated by a good stretch of broad, firm track, until the Open Access land extends north to take in the old railway near Ay Gill; from here the track can be followed to the cutting where the boundary fence is reached.

Across the cutting the fence climbs up a rise and the boundary stones begin again. Near the top of the rise the second stone is numbered 49 but the style of numbering is different from those across Mickle Fell and Lunedale. Further on another is number 38; all others are more roughly shaped and blank. The terrain levels out, the fence heads south and the going is very squelchy; after crossing the small valley of Ay Gill, where a shooting hut appears on the right, it becomes merely squelchy. When I went over in July the cross-leaved heath was coming into flower. Of the three main types of heather found on the northern hills this is the first to show its pinkish colours; it generally prefers wetter areas. It is soon followed by the deep purple bell heather and finally in August vast acreages of ling spread a purple carpet across the moors.

Soon Tan Hill Inn can be seen in the distance. Before that comes Ease Gill which may be an awkward crossing. If the water is too deep the best thing is to head upstream where, just before the road is reached, fording it should be easier. It's then a short walk along the road to the cattle grid and county boundary signs at Tackan Tan and a slightly longer walk from there to the pub – and may the bar be open!

Tan Hill

What is there to say about Tan Hill? What is there *not* to say about Tan Hill? There is in fact so much that it's difficult to know where to start. I could of course start with its most famous feature, the Tan Hill Inn; but what about the name? Let's start with the name.

Derived from the Celtic, *tân* is the modern Welsh word for fire and *heol* means street, road or lane. The term *tân heol* (Celtic 'road of fire') is used at Carnac in Brittany in connection with bonfires lit at midsummer.[1] Alfred Watkins, who investigated ley lines in the 1920s, claimed to have identified many such lines which terminated at hilltop points with names signifying beacon sites and quoted the prime example of what was believed to be the highest point on the Wiltshire Downs, also called Tan Hill, thus relating the beacon fire to an ancient 'way'.[2] Many people scoff at the idea of ley lines and other spiritual or supernatural phenomena (Watkins was derided in his own time). I have an open mind. How does one explain the familiar art of water divining for instance, which I have seen demonstrated although I couldn't make it work myself? I consider that the ancient people had far more knowledge than we give them credit for, knowledge which is lost to us because we no longer have an intimate connection with the earth and nature, knowledge which those in the scientific community dismiss because they don't understand it and perhaps don't want to try. This makes these mysterious beliefs much more fascinating for me than the clinical, organised, documented and ultimately boring Romans.

There is, however, an unfortunate flaw in Watkins' choice of example as a new survey in 2009 confirmed a suspicion held by some that the highest point on the Wiltshire Downs is not Tan Hill but nearby Milk Hill which is about ten inches (yes, inches) higher – trust modern science to spoil a good legend! A few barrow loads of stone, topsoil and turf should sort it.

However, it may still be that this high point on the Pennines, *Tân Heol*,

---

1 Robertson, Dawn, and Koronka, Peter, *op. cit.*, 1992.
2 Watkins, Alfred, *The Old Straight Track*, New Edn, Head of Zeus Ltd., 2014 (originally published 1925)

was used by the Celts as a beacon site. There is no proof of it but certainly a large fire here would have been visible for miles. This brings us neatly to the pub, which in the 1970s was virtually destroyed by fire on more than one occasion.

If anywhere along the 'North West Frontier' can be termed an icon it is this lonely, isolated, windswept border station. At over 1,730 feet the Tan Hill Inn is Britain's highest pub. It dates from the late seventeenth or early eighteenth century, although William Camden apparently referred to a previous inn here in 1586, and it was no doubt built to serve the cattle drovers and packhorse trains which passed this way and the miners at the nearby pits, for coal and lead were extracted here, the former from at least the fourteenth century, the latter as far back as Roman times.

A small group of cottages also once stood here but these were demolished in the mid-twentieth century after the mines closed. The coal, known as 'crow' coal, was poor quality, producing a lot of soot, and became uneconomic when the superior products of the Durham coalfields could be more easily accessed.

The inn is described as 'world famous', probably with good reason as it has featured in television adverts for double glazing, gone into battle with Kentucky Fried Chicken over trading name issues (a battle from which Kentucky Fried Chicken withdrew in confused humiliation) and been a regular subject for the media who, always ready for good bad weather stories, have eagerly reported on the plight (or delight) of parties stranded there by snowdrifts. It has even entered the world of theoretical physics, featuring in a recent BBC4 series, *Gravity and Me: The Force That Shapes Our Lives*, presented by Jim Al-Khalili, much of which went straight over my head. Obviously the force of gravity was insufficient to make it penetrate my brain!

As the mines became unprofitable and the packhorse and droving trades declined in the face of competition from better road transport and the railways the inn too fell on hard times and for several years at the beginning of the twentieth century lay semi-derelict until in 1903 Richard and Susan Parrington took it over and brought it back to life. Susan refused to leave for the birth of their third daughter in 1906, making a typically blunt Yorkshire remark that has gone down in the history and folklore of the pub: 'Ah were tupped theer an' Ahs'll lamb theer!'

Following Richard's untimely death she married Michael Peacock and remained a legendary and formidable landlady, once seeing off an unwel-

Tan Hill Inn.

come customer with her husband's service revolver, until her own death in 1936. She is buried in the little churchyard at Keld.

In more recent times one of her successors gained fame (or notoriety, depending on one's point of view) by being dubbed 'the rudest landlady in Britain'. I was present on one occasion when she gave a small demonstration of how she got the title, although it wasn't directed at me. Neil Hanson, who served two terms as landlord, first as a tenant in the late 1970s then as owner in the mid-1980s, has written two highly entertaining books recounting his experiences with the often likeable, frequently disreputable, occasionally obnoxious and sometimes downright eccentric clientele and detailing much history in the process. At no time does he actually name 'the Inn at the Top', or any other place in the locality for that matter, but all are immediately identifiable by anyone with even a 'middling' knowledge of the area.[3]

It's not my place to say any more than I already have so instead I will relate a story which involved me personally and which has at least a slight

---

3 Hanson, Neil, *The Inn At The Top: Tales of Life at the Highest Pub in Britain*, Michael O' Mara Books, 2013, and *Pigs Might Fly: More Dales Tales*, Dale Publishing, 2015.

connection with the pub in that I'd just been in there when it happened (it was nothing to do with the drink, I hasten to add). It will also serve as a cautionary tale for anyone who walks these high Pennine moors, especially alone.

Coming up from Keld the Pennine Way makes a bee-line for the inn until at the road it crosses diagonally to a stile which leads onto Sleightholme Moor. Curiously at this point most walkers seem to lose their ability to read a map or guide book and carry on straight ahead, thus ending up in the bar – a simple mistake, easily made.

It was a beautiful sunny day, mild and pleasant although it was early November. I'd travelled by bus from Darlington via Richmond and Reeth to Keld, intending to do no more than follow the Pennine Way up to Tan Hill and back but it was a 'good to be alive' day and I decided to head on to Bowes. This would probably mean a further four-mile walk along a busy main road to Barnard Castle to catch a bus home but the weather was so glorious I didn't care. So having treated myself to lunch in the pub I set off cheerily in the direction of Bowes.

Now this stretch of the Pennine Way, like many others, has something of a reputation for being boggy and it was certainly squelchy underfoot, but there was nothing to suggest that any particular part was wetter than any other until, without even a split-second's warning, I went in up to my chest. I think my rucksack stopped me going further in as my feet weren't touching the bottom.

I didn't panic but I knew I was in trouble. There was no-one else around. The pub had disappeared from view. I had no foothold and only scraps of loose vegetation to hold on to. Cautiously I leaned forward until I could rest against something which felt reasonably firm, then probing gently with my toes I slowly pushed myself upwards so that I could reach out to grasp some stronger heather shoots. Little by little I eased myself out and finally, after what seemed like an hour but was probably only about ten minutes, I was able to get to my feet.

Standing there, dripping wet, covered in mud and weeds, I actually laughed, mostly from relief but partly at the thought that had I gone in over my head I might have been preserved in the peat and become a bog body, to be dug up in five thousand years' time and exhibited in a museum as a specimen of *Homo Ambulensis*.

As there was no-one in sight I took off my wet gear and, ironically, put on my waterproofs. The walk was obviously over for the day so I made my way to the Arkengarthdale road and set off for Reeth, knowing that I would miss the bus to Richmond but still feeling quite jaunty, confident of getting home somehow. But after half a mile or so of walking in wet socks and boots I decided to do something I've rarely done in the past and thumbed a lift. To my surprise the first car to pass pulled up and a very kind couple took me to Reeth where I was in good time for the bus. Not wishing to admit defeat I went back the following week and did the walk again, this time without mishap.

The moral, of course, is don't get complacent or over-confident; carry walking poles and use them to probe carefully on any suspect ground; and please, please tell someone where you are going!

Before returning to the boundary we must say something about the local inhabitants. No, not the people, there are precious few of them – the sheep, of course, and the red grouse.

Throughout the Pennines the predominant breed of sheep is the Swaledale. Derived from the same original stock as other hill breeds, Dalesbred, Rough Fell and Blackface, with their long, thick wool and

Swaledale sheep.

distinctive black and white faces, they are extremely hardy, well able to cope with the harsh winter conditions, even capable of surviving buried under snowdrifts, sometimes for several days. Their other claim to fame is that the ewes make exceedingly good mothers. They are found everywhere and have a particular connection with Tan Hill. In 1919 the Swaledale Sheep Breeders' Association was formed by farmers from the area, shows were arranged and although they were discontinued for a time they were reinstated in 1951 and a major event has been held at Tan Hill ever since. The prizes at such shows are in themselves worth little; it is the kudos which comes with winning that counts for it can add many thousands of pounds to an animal's value. The record price for a Swaledale tup, set in 2002, is £101,000.[4]

Vast acreages of the Pennines are maintained as grouse moors. Like all blood sports grouse shooting is a highly contentious and emotive matter, arousing strong passions and seemingly irreconcilable opinions. Not long ago the BBC's *Countryfile* programme screened a report on the subject, presenting arguments from both sides. This is not the place to get involved in the debate; I mention shooting only because it takes place on so much of the land we are crossing. I will merely list very briefly some of the issues and point out an observation from the past.

The case for:-
- it provides local employment;
- it contributes millions of pounds to the rural economy;
- it promotes effective management of moorlands which would otherwise revert to scrubland.

The case against:-
- it may result in a conflict of interest over land use between shooting and sheep-farming
- in some parts of the country it has resulted in the illegal destruction of predators including endangered birds of prey;
- the dominant practice of 'driven' shoots (beaters driving the birds towards a line of guns) over 'point' shoots (dogs flushing out the birds) results in much higher kills;
- the management regime, particularly heather burning on environmentally sensitive areas, damages the peat bogs and harms wildlife.

---

4 www.swaledale-sheep.com

Listening to the rhetoric and reading through the propaganda and bearing in mind the old saying that truth is the first casualty of war, one can ask of the 'for' arguments 'but does it really?' and of the 'against' arguments 'but are things really that bad?' One must draw one's own conclusions. I make no further comment on the rights and wrongs, if they can be described as such, except to refer again to Edmund Bogg who, remember, was writing in the late 1890s. On the subject of Swaledale 'characters' he mentions George Reynoldson, then in his eighties, who was called as a witness in a court case over shooting rights. Questioned by the judge on some aspect of shooting, old George replied:

> Yer Honour, it isn't shutting noo-a-days, it's on'y modder! When Ah were a lad, gentlemen use to shut ower points – that's wat A' call sport. Noo-a-days, t'gents hire men to draave birds tit guns, which is nowt at all but modder![5]

The view not of some twenty-first century city-born animal rights activist but of a true homespun dalesman of more than one hundred and twenty years ago.

What follows now is not pleasant but it needs to be told. It arises out of an incident which occurred after I had drafted this chapter. At the time it made me very angry and I originally wrote this additional account with a pen dipped in vitriol. Now the anger has been replaced by a feeling more of sadness and disappointment so I have moderated my tone.

Shortly before Christmas 2016 (17 December to be precise) I left the Keld-Nateby road to walk a shooters' track up Little Sleddale towards Gregory Chapel above the Mallerstang Valley. The map shows this track running a couple of miles or so into the hills then ending perhaps half a mile from the top. Not having walked it before I intended it as a reconnaissance for a longer walk to be undertaken at a more suitable time of year so the plan was to reach the end of the track and return.

Sure enough I came to a turning area where motor vehicles could go no further. It was a nice fine day and before leaving I decided it was a good place to have some lunch. At least, it would have been were it not for what I found there.

Dog shit – not just the odd turd but several piles of the stuff, and large piles at that, in the grass around the edge of the turning circle. I make no

---

5 Bogg, Edmund, op. cit., 1909

apology for the basic language or the graphic description – they serve to convey my disgust. It didn't take Sherlock Holmes to pinpoint who was responsible. This is a remote place – few walkers would come this way, certainly not with enough dogs to cause so much mess. Nor was it a farmer with his sheepdog. It was a far larger party with several dogs – grouse shooters, no less. I had in fact seen a shoot in progress on this track only a few weeks earlier. To avoid mistake the grid reference of this canine latrine is NY814003. Its remoteness is irrelevant – it should not have been left in such a state. I find it dispiriting that it was left so, and by those whom one would expect to behave more responsibly. So to any of them who may be reading this, I hope it's pricked a conscience or two. You know who you are and where it is. In future, show some respect and clean it up – other people use the paths and the countryside.

Returning to more wholesome matters, what of the boundary around these parts? In the past it did some odd things. Palmer refers to it as performing 'a double-crossing diagram' and older maps show that it ran back and forth across the road three times in about 400 yards between Tackan Tan and the West Stonesdale road end. I have failed to discover the reason for this strange zig-zag, compressed as it is into such a small area. When the Yorkshire Dales National Park was designated in 1954 its boundary too followed this quirky line, although the county boundary was amended in 1988, transferring to North Yorkshire a small section of road previously isolated in Cumbria. The county boundary now runs to the north-east of the road. The origins of the zig-zag appear to be lost in time; I could find no reference to it in the County Record Offices. An enquiry at the National Park Office in Bainbridge, however, resulted in a telephone conversation with David Butterworth, the Park's Chief Executive. He told me that the procedure for changing a county boundary is relatively straightforward; that for changing a national park boundary is not. When the county boundary was straightened in 1988 the National Park Committee were asked if they wanted the park boundary to be amended to coincide and they said 'Yes please', otherwise a small triangle of land would be moved from Cumbria into North Yorkshire but would be excluded from the park. The bureaucracy and administration were such, however, that it proved impractical, so the park boundary continues to follow its original course. Funny things, boundaries; are they deliberately devised to cause problems?

The other, far more contentious, issue here was the shifting of the County

Durham boundary southwards all the way from Teesdale to the road at Tan Hill, thus including the pub within the new line, to the outrage of the locals. Not only had Yorkshire lost its highest summit but its highest pub too.

I said earlier that some of the 1974 changes made sense; this one was just plain barmy. If the purpose of transferring the northernmost parts of Yorkshire was to facilitate their service from Barnard Castle rather than, say, Richmond, the place to draw the new line was along the A66. The nearest village to Tan Hill within the new County Durham was Bowes, seven miles away along a very minor road and a rough track suitable only for 4x4s; the route from Barnard Castle, eleven miles away as the curlew flies, lay over the Stang into Arkengarthdale (twelve miles) from where it was a further eight miles to the pub. A forty mile round trip just to empty the bins from a single property! But some Whitehall bureaucrat, with no idea of the local geography, thought the road would make a good boundary and drew his line on the map accordingly. The result was that Durham County Council had to pay North Yorkshire County Council to carry out services on their behalf. Bonkers. This situation persisted until 1991 when the Boundary Commission finally saw sense and returned the Tan Hill Inn to its rightful place.

I've spent a lot of time talking about Tan Hill because of its local significance. Also it's almost half way along the 'North West Frontier' and one of only three places where there is habitation and a chance of accommodation. Now we must press on; but we haven't finished with the boundary conflicts around here – oh no, not by a long way.

Boundary stone on the Barras to Tan Hill road.

Tan Hill to Nine Standards Rigg – the Lyell-Hothfield Boundary Dispute

When this book was in its very early planning stages and when my ideas of how to proceed were still quite vague I was intrigued by the unusual line of the boundary north-west of Tan Hill Inn referred to in the last chapter. Why did it do that? I was also interested in two observations which Palmer makes when describing the route between Tan Hill and Nine Standards Rigg.

Firstly he mentions a boundary stone bearing the inscription 'LH 1912' which he assumes denotes Lord Hothfield's estate. This stone is still there by the roadside and there are others along the way, as I discovered. Secondly he states that the boundary follows a 'Judgment Line' running due west towards Backstone Beck Foot (also called Beck Meetings). Judgment for what, I wondered?

This line is obvious on the Explorer map and also on some older OS editions. But even a quick consultation of the 1862 six inch map reveals a completely different picture. From Tackan Tan the boundary is the same as at present, roughly south-west along Cocklake Rigg, but whereas today it turns to take a dead-straight course due west, the old line runs north-west to Hugh Seat Nab, makes its way to Brownber Tarn, then meanders and zig-zags south-west towards the southern end of Nine Standards Rigg. Thus it appears that at some time in

Boundary stone inscribed LH 1912.

the late nineteenth or early twentieth centuries a significant area of land was transferred from the North Riding of Yorkshire to Westmorland. Why?

Examination of papers, maps, press reports and county council minutes in the Record Offices at Kendal, Durham and Northallerton brought to light an absorbing if rather involved story which I will try to outline without getting bogged down (I use the term deliberately) in too much legal detail. Quotations and other information used here are by permission of Durham County Record Office, North Yorkshire County Record Office and Cumbria Archives Service as detailed in the footnotes.

As mentioned earlier, the indeterminate nature of the boundaries in these upland areas led to much dispute and litigation. In the early 1900s matters reached a head when a long-standing issue over common and grazing rights was revived between Captain Francis Horner Lyell, Lord of the Manor of Muker (in Yorkshire) and Henry James Tufton, 1st Baron Hothfield, Lord of the Manors of Winton and Kaber (in Westmorland). The Board of Agriculture & Fisheries set up an inquiry to settle the matter, presided over by an assistant commissioner, a barrister named G. Pemberton Leach, and held initially at Kirkby Stephen, beginning in June 1912. Mr. J. Ingram Dawson, solicitor of Barnard Castle, represented the owners of farms in Upper Swaledale, Mr. Hudson, solicitor of Richmond, represented Captain Lyell, and Mr. Rankin, barrister of London, represented Lord Hothfield. Westmorland County Council was also represented but strangely for a matter which concerned the location of the county boundary the North Riding County Council was not.

In his opening address Mr. Rankin stated that entitlement to the manors had descended through the centuries and the original grant deeds had been lost. He had documentary evidence going back to 1617 and details of the boundary perambulations from 1651 to 1896. There had been uncertainty and differences of opinion from at least the beginning of the eighteenth century and the area in dispute had increased over time. There was a marked discrepancy between Captain Lyell's interpretation of the boundary line and Lord Hothfield's; it was said to be 'the water deal' but at certain points what was claimed to be the watershed was incorrect.[1] Having been up there myself I can see that determining its actual course would be very difficult. As will be shown in the next chapter the watershed is between not two river systems but three; the ground is rugged in the extreme and deciding in the

---

[1] Durham County Record Office, D/HH6/6/1-70

midst of the morass which way a small sluggish rivulet might be running would be almost impossible.

The question turned primarily on land use: who had used it, how they had used it and for how long, and if they were actually entitled to do so. Numerous witnesses were called, mainly gamekeepers and shepherds, many of them elderly and of long local standing, who gave evidence on these points. If the lawyers involved had only a sketchy idea of upland management at the beginning of the hearing, by the time it ended in October they were experts.

Despite the underlying seriousness of the issue, the proceedings appear to have been carried out with some humour, comments being made about the relationships between the witnesses, the sagacity of the sheep in their ability to know where they should and should not be, and so on. Several paragraphs in the press reports conclude with the observation 'Laughter'.

Mr. Leach found in favour of Lord Hothfield; it turned out that at previous hearings in 1843 and 1847 the Tithe Commissioner, Mr. M. Mathew, had made similar awards, neither of which had been set aside by the High Court but which both parties had in practice completely disregarded. Nevertheless Mr. Leach was of the opinion that they were conclusive and binding and declined to find otherwise. He must, however, have anticipated that his decision would be contested as he directed that only temporary boundary markers should be placed until the award was confirmed.[1] The presence today of the boundary stones, clearly inscribed 'LH 1912', indicates that it was confirmed despite the objections outlined below. Those are the basic facts of the case, put as succinctly as possible.

The fall-out from the decision was considerable. The boundary was moved between half a mile and a mile southwards and Yorkshire lost some eight hundred acres to Westmorland. The Yorkshire press was indignant, to say the least. *The Yorkshire Herald* of the 24 October 1912 regarded the transfer as:

> a rather remarkable proceeding... by a stroke of a pen of a *not very important official* a number of Swaledale farmers find themselves without fell pasturage.[1]

(The italics are the author's but in the copy in Durham County Record Office someone has underlined these words in ink).

---

[1] Durham County Record Office, D/HH6/6/1-70

Although there was no resident population it was strange that the county area should be altered without a judicial inquiry. Regarding this, reference was made to the North Riding Quarter Sessions, reported in the *Yorkshire Post* of the 18 October, when the Chairman of the Quarter Sessions expressed the opinion that the transfer ought not to be done without such an inquiry at which the Quarter Sessions or the inhabitants of the North Riding, through the North Riding County Council, would have a say. (One wonders why this was not done in the first place). He believed that as Quarter Sessions Chairman he had a right of veto on the alteration but was unsure of his precise legal standing and was doubtful about using the veto unless he had the full support of his colleagues. A resolution was passed giving him their backing.[1]

On the 26 December the *Herald* again reported that:

> the well-known dale of Swaledale can no longer be said to be wholly in the County of York and many farms situate in this district will be seriously affected for if the Assistant Commissioner's award is allowed to stand unchallenged they will be deprived of pasturage which they have hitherto enjoyed upon this tract of land... it is believed that the Council of the North Riding has not lost sight of the question.[2]

Indeed, at their meeting on the 30 October, the North Riding County Council had resolved:

> that with reference to the boundaries of certain manors and parishes within the North Riding of Yorkshire and the County of Westmorland now the subject of an arbitration before an Assistant Commissioner of the Board of Agriculture & Fisheries, the county council do oppose any alteration being made to the boundary of the North Riding as shown on the ordnance map, and that the Finance Committee be instructed to take all such steps as they think necessary or desirable in the matter.[3]

In fact it appears that the council got cold feet; they threw in the towel, no appeal was lodged and there is no further reference to the issue in the minutes. A letter dated 22 January 1913 from Mr. J. Ingram Dawson to the Clerk of North Riding County Council is telling. It reads:

> I duly received your letter of the 21st inst. and note that the County Council

---

1 Durham County Record Office, D/HH6/6/1-70
2 North Yorkshire County Record Office, NRCC/CL1/727
3 North Yorkshire County Record Office, NRCC/C/1/1/8

are not taking any steps as to the appeal. I am afraid no action can be taken later. *I am afraid the inhabitants of Swaledale will be greatly disappointed, as they are intensely Yorkshire and resent greatly the idea of eight or nine hundred acres being transferred to Westmorland.*[2] (author's italics).

The only reference to the case in the Westmorland County Council minutes is dated the 22 November 1913 where it was reported that the Ordnance Survey had enquired if Westmorland County Council concurred in the adoption of the manor boundaries between Winton, Kaber and Muker as the boundaries of the parishes and counties also, following the award of the Assistant Commissioner. It was submitted that this interpretation was correct.[4]

There the matter rested, at least as far as the boundary was concerned. The 1919 edition of the six inch OS map shows it as it exists today.

But it was not quite the end of the legal wrangling. Captain Lyell let the boundary issue drop but there remained the question of rights of common over the land between the old and the new boundaries. Once more the case of Lyell v Hothfield appeared in the court proceedings for June 1914.[1]

The result does not appear in the papers in Durham County Record Office, at least not in those I have examined, and I have not pursued it further (I guess that Lord Hothfield won) as it did not involve the boundary and anyway it was of little consequence in the light of what happened in the wider world only a few weeks later.

It is interesting to note that at the time of the original inquiry in 1912 Mr. Ingram Dawson, besides representing those opposed to Lord Hothfield, was involved in his own dispute with his Lordship regarding two farms which he, i.e. Mr. Dawson, owned near Brough and for which he claimed grazing rights on Winton and Kaber Fells. Here too, although the county boundary was not in question, Lord Hothfield was successful.[5]

It is easy to portray Lord Hothfield as a greedy, grasping, aristocratic landowner, but it was pointed out during the hearings that he was in fact a caring landlord, fighting for the rights of his tenants, rights which they had enjoyed for many, many years. The same could no doubt be said of Captain Lyell. But the decision had to be made; whether it was the correct one we

---

2 North Yorkshire County Record Office, NRCC/CL1/727
4 Cumbria Archives Service, Kendal, WC/C/1
1 Durham County Record Office, D/HH6/6/1-70
5 Cumbria Archives Service, Kendal, WDHH/50

can now only speculate. We shall meet Lord Hothfield again, or rather, his ancestors, later.

I have described this episode in some detail because it is a clear illustration of how the county boundary has not been a fixed, immoveable feature through the centuries and how its lack of accurate definition caused long-term problems. It also shows how divisive such matters can be; if the transfer of a small parcel of remote, rough moorland, uninhabited except by sheep and wildlife, can arouse such indignation and resentment, how much more contentious is the large-scale dismemberment of an entire county to satisfy the whims of the ivory tower-dwelling bureaucrats?

Tan Hill to Nine Standards Rigg – The Route

So what of the route along this 'Judgment Line' which caused so much trouble and no doubt a great deal of expense? I don't want to put people off (wouldn't dream of doing such a thing), but it is fair to give warning that although it's only about five miles, four of them are very tough going, so much so that it took me three attempts, two from the east and one from the west, before I got across.

As I mentioned in the last chapter, this area is the watershed between three river systems. To the north, Bleaberry Beck and Great and Little Stowgill form the headwaters of the River Belah which joins the Eden between Kirkby Stephen and Brough, the ultimate destination being the Solway Firth and the Irish Sea; to the north-east, Ease Gill first becomes White Stone Gill, then Sleightholme Beck before running into the River Greta, then the Tees, reaching the North Sea at Teesmouth; and to the south, the waters of Whitsundale Beck and its tributaries make their long journey to the North Sea via the Swale, the Ure, the Ouse and finally the mighty Humber, at the very most opposite, most distant corner of Yorkshire.

If a raindrop could choose, which way would it go? The answer is that many don't go anywhere – they stay where they fall. I'm sure some mathematician has devised a formula to predict how long it will take a raindrop to reach the sea. If so, I'm equally sure he didn't make his calculations on the sodden wastes of Winton and Kaber Fells.

On my first attempt I started from Tan Hill intending to reach Nine Standards Rigg and return via Whitsundale and Ravenseat but as I quickly discovered I had set off too late in the morning. The first mile or so south-west along Cocklake Rigg is not too bad but when the boundary turns due west to follow the Judgment Line the trouble starts. It took me half an hour to cover less than two hundred yards. Palmer calls it 'wickedly bad country' and he's dead right. If the bogs below Mickle Fell are Purgatory, those along here are Hades itself. The peat groughs are deep, wet and unavoidable; ascending and descending are equally slippery, slithery, mucky jobs. Realising that there was no chance of reaching the Nine Standards in the

Ravenseat.

time available, let alone completing the whole round, I turned back.

I've often found that if a route presents difficulties or if the path is hard to find or follow it pays to try it from the opposite end – it is frequently much more obvious. So a few weeks later I left Kirkby Stephen for the Nine Standards, intent on heading east down to Beck Meetings at the head of Whitsundale and from there along the Judgment Line to Tan Hill. The previous weeks had been mild and dry and the notorious eroded peat south of the Nine Standards was not a problem. But heading down Near Grains the ground was broken up by tributary streams separated by high banks of peat. It soon became clear that once more I had left it too late so again I retreated. I'll say more about this occasion later as it had a very significant outcome.

If at first you don't succeed...

On the third attempt I left Tan Hill much earlier, determined this time to complete the round. In the meantime I had actually done part of it by walking from Ravenseat, up Whitsundale, then up the course of Backstone Beck to Nine Standards Rigg and found it reasonably straightforward. The fence which serves as a guide all the way from Maize Beck ends at Beck Meetings but then it's relatively easy going up a gradual slope. Only near the top is there likely to be confusion in poor visibility as the tributary streams which deterred me previously make it difficult to judge which course to follow. In such conditions a compass is essential. Otherwise there are glimpses of the Nine Standards, then a signpost comes into view on the ridge, marking the route of the Coast to Coast Walk, and this is the point to aim for.

So with at least some knowledge of what lay ahead I set out from Tan Hill once more. I soon found the first of the 'LH 1912' boundary stones. But the going, as before, was slow and arduous. With uneasy memories of Sleightholme Moor I probed carefully among the grass, reeds and moss and at one point my pole sank a good two feet into an unseen, water-filled hollow. Regardless of the environmental benefits I began to question whether peat bogs were in fact ultimately for my own good. More boundary stones, more peat hags, then the way along the fence was obstructed by a huge area of reeds. Reed beds can be a boon or a bane. Treading on them can assist in getting over wet patches but at the same time they conceal those wet patches and care is required in choosing where to put one's feet as the water can be of some depth. I tried to get around this one until I realised that its enormous size was pushing me directly away from the fence. Cursing Lord Hothfield and his bloody boundary dispute I headed back into the reeds, squelching slowly onwards to regain the fence. At last I began the descent to Beck Meetings and from there I returned to Tan Hill via Ravenseat.

Lest anyone should think 'Oh, it can't be as bad as all that', let me refer again to two writers, one from the past, one from the present, whom I have mentioned before – Edmund Bogg and Andrew Bibby. Bogg crossed slightly further south, from the ruined 'watcher's' (gamekeeper's) shelter of Robert's Seat House to the head of Whitsundale and on to Nine Standards Rigg:

> A wild rugged waste… we toil perilously onwards knee-deep in wiry ling, scrub or treacherous black-brown peat… It is a most fatiguing walk… full of haggs, pits and rifts or gullies like the crevasses of a glacier, their depth ten to fifteen feet, and as wide… only a stride or two of level ground separates them.[1]

Bibby, going in the opposite direction, following the watershed further north, describes it as a 'potentially hazardous undertaking' and in doing so

---

1 Bogg, Edmund – *op. cit.*, 1909.

Ravenseat – the packhorse bridge over Whitsundale Beck.

he was aware of the possibility of falling into one of the disused mineshafts.[2] This is a danger which I've so far omitted to mention, but much of the Pennines is littered with these old abandoned workings, even in the wildest, most remote places, and the danger is real. This is not an area to be treated lightly; the Pennines don't take prisoners.

Before saying something about the tiny settlement of Ravenseat there is one further story from history which needs to be told. This is a dispute of a very different kind, the ill-fated Kaber Rigg Plot.

After the restoration of Charles II in 1660 there was an attempted insurrection aimed at deposing him and reinstating the Commonwealth. Captain Robert Atkinson of Mallerstang had served in the Parliamentary army during the Civil War and had attained significant rank, commanding troops in Westmorland and becoming Governor of Appleby. (Throughout the Civil War Appleby was staunchly Royalist; nearby Kirkby Stephen was equally strongly Parliamentarian. I understand that the differences have not been entirely forgotten). In October 1663 Captain Atkinson took part in what was planned as a national uprising, gathering a small party of supporters on Kaber Rigg. But the affair was a fiasco; the expected reinforcements

---

2 Bibby, Andrew – *op. cit.*, 2008.

never arrived and faced with a purposeless night on the cold moorland, they abandoned the enterprise and dispersed. They were betrayed to the Royalist authorities and Captain Atkinson was later executed for treason.[2]

While Ravenseat is situated in a remote side valley reached by a minor road branching off an only slightly less minor road, it is far from lonely. It is a popular spot not only with walkers but with motor-borne visitors too, for besides being on the Coast to Coast Walk it is the home of Clive and Amanda Owen who have become well-known – one might even say famous – for their numerous appearances on television and Amanda's books relating the story of how she came to Ravenseat and her subsequent life as shepherdess to both flock and family in the high Pennines.[3]

The name Ravenseat is derived from the Norse *hrafn* (raven) and *saetr* (summer pasture). Like Grains o' th' Beck it was much larger in past times; in 1820 there were five farms, a chapel and a population of 88. The renowned Yorkshire chroniclers Marie Hartley and Joan Ingilby note that at a court case in 1788 a witness named Mary Moore, who was then aged 66, declared that her father had kept an inn there.[4] The footpath from the west, now one of the Coast to Coast routes, was an important packhorse or drovers' road between Kirkby Stephen and Barnard Castle, known as a 'jagger' road. The jagger was the leader of the packhorse train, the name coming from the German Jaeger-Galloway ponies used by the packmen.[5]

They perhaps used this route to avoid paying tolls on the Barras-Tan Hill road which was turnpiked around 1770. The old hump-backed packhorse bridge still spans Whitsundale Beck close to the farm. Coal from Tan Hill was carried this way and many people earned a living by knitting woollen stockings, an occupation carried on in other parts of the Dales, notably Dentdale and Upper Wensleydale, as well as in the upper Eden and Lune valleys – Kirkby Stephen was an important stocking market.

In March 1664 John Smith, a stocking merchant, left Ravenseat for Nateby carrying a large sum of money. His body was found two years later at a place near the Keld-Nateby road called Hawkinge Bower. James Alderson and his two sons, of Thwaite, were accused of the murder by James Hutchinson of

---

2 Bibby, Andrew – *op. cit.*, 2008.
3 Owen, Amanda – *The Yorkshire Shepherdess*, Sidgwick & Jackson, 2014; *A Year in the Life of the Yorkshire Shepherdess*, Sidgwick & Jackson, 2016.
4 Hartley, Marie and Ingilby, Joan – *A Dales Heritage: Life Stories from Documents and Folk Memory*, Dalesman Publishing Co., 1982.
5 Wright, Geoffrey N. – op. cit., 1985.

TAN HILL TO NINE STANDARDS RIGG – THE ROUTE

Eighteenth century Smardale Bridge over Scandale Beck – a long way from the county boundary but once the site of an inn, reputedly a meeting place of the Kaber Rigg plotters. . .

Hartley, who it is believed was the real culprit, but the case was dropped through lack of evidence.[6] Hawkinge Bower is now known as Blue John Holes, blue being the predominant colour of the victim's goods.

Ravenseat has its waterfalls – High Force, which can in no way rival its namesake in Teesdale, and the more enigmatic Jenny Whaley Falls. Who was Jenny Whaley? No-one knows. Was she a wise woman, soothsayer or witch, like Knaresborough's Mother Shipton? Or, like Janet who lived behind Janet's Foss near Gordale Scar, a water sprite, responsible perhaps for bewitching a man named Edward Cleasby of Muker, who disappeared mysteriously, never to be seen again? Or a doomed lover like the Singing Lady, but possibly with sinister attributes, as was Sarkless Kitty of Farndale? ('Sarkless' Kitty Garthwaite was a real person; for proof that truth can be stranger than fiction read her tragic story and its remarkable sequel in John Hillaby's *Journey Home*).[7]

---

6 Hartley, Marie and Ingilby, Joan, *op. cit.* 1982.
7 Hillaby, John – Journey Home, Constable & Co., 1983.

Moor Close is a lonely farm, now long abandoned and derelict, standing on the hillside west of Thwaite, near the Pennine Way as it descends from Great Shunner Fell. Edmund Bogg writes of its then occupant, another old Swaledale 'character' called Jamie Calvert, known as Moor Close Jamie. According to Bogg, Jamie fancied that:

> Theer's a muckle o' brass hid up at t' top o' Swardal. When ah were a lad foaks didn't put ther brass i' t' banks! Noo, theer wer aude Jock Duke – he hed lots o' brass, an' when he deed, suddent, theer were nivver ony clue to what becam on it… [there's] a vast o' wealth hidden somwheer i' Sleddal or Nine Stanners Rigg.[8]

So with the tantalising prospect of finding buried treasure we reach those strange, baffling structures known as the Nine Standards where Dr. Stephen Walker is certain there are other exciting discoveries to be made.

---

8 Bogg, Edmund – *op. cit.*, 1909.

The Nine Standards

Currick, currack, hurrock, cairn, carn – just some of the terms used on maps and in documents to denote the numerous stone edifices found throughout the northern Pennines. The appearances of these constructions are as different as the names used to describe them. Some are just piles of stones, large or small, heaped together in varying degrees of tidiness. Others, though carefully built in the manner of drystone walling, assume equally assorted shapes and sizes. They are found singly, in groups, in lines, on hilltops, on ridges, on plateaux. Some act as boundary markers, some as guide posts. The purpose of others is often more obscure. They may be ancient, or at least historic, or more modern, and may be continually evolving as today's walkers follow the long-established tradition of adding a stone to any they pass.

None, however, come close to matching the Nine Standards in number, variety, style, arrangement or complete lack of clues as to their *raison d'être*. No-one knows when the Nine Standards were built, why they were built or who built them. The ravages of time have necessitated rebuilding on occasions, most recently in 2005, but they have become so ingrained into the landscape around Kirkby Stephen that people just accept them – 'Oh, they've always been there' – giving rise perhaps to some sort of belief that, like Topsy in *Uncle Tom's Cabin*, they 'jest growed'.

This has led inevitably to a number of popular and oft-quoted legends about their origins, the two foremost being that they were intended to scare off Scottish raiders by presenting the appearance of an army camped on the ridge, or were merely the handiwork of shepherds with time to spare, neither of which has any basis in fact.

Dr. Stephen Walker, a native of the area, set out several years ago to try and discover more about these lithological enigmas. I don't propose to examine here his convincing arguments for their ancient origins or the detailed research which led to his conclusions. These can be studied in his book *The Nine Standards: Ancient Cairns or Modern Folly?*[1] and an account of the technical survey work undertaken since its publication is available on

---

1 Walker, Stephen – *op. cit.*, 2008.

the Friends of the Nine Standards website;[2] but as they are so close to the boundary I have to make some observations of my own.

Nine stone cairns, large and substantially built, obviously designed to last, standing in a line on a ridge overlooking a broad valley, of ancient, possibly prehistoric, origin – surely a classic place to find a ley line? Alfred Watkins, preoccupied as he was with southern England, makes no reference to the Nine Standards. The well-known authorities on the ancient, the extraordinary and the spiritual, Janet and Colin Bord, also disregard them. Their *Guide to Ancient Sites in Britain* does not mention them and a search for 'Nine Standards' on their website results in a blank screen.

John Timpson, the former BBC broadcaster, who investigated ley lines in a more light-hearted way, also omits them from his book *Timpson's Ley Lines: A Layman Tracking the Leys*. These omissions are not surprising. The writers have most likely fallen into the trap of believing that because no-one prior to Dr. Walker has thought to seriously investigate the Nine Standards they cannot be of ancient origin and are merely a local curiosity with no real significance. But surely they should merit inclusion in John Timpson's other book, *Timpson's England: A Look Beyond the Obvious*, which contains oddities of all types, many of which are well-known and documented and by no means of any great age. After all, he does mention the Tan Hill Inn, from where the Nine Standards are clearly visible.

There are numerous archaeological sites in and around the Eden Valley but I certainly do not have the knowledge or ability to link them to the Nine Standards via a ley line. I found it somewhat surprising that no-one else had done so until Stephen Walker told me that he believes it has in fact been done, the 'target areas' being around Shap, although it seems this work has never been written up. Also the stone circles at Gamelands, east of Orton, and Long Meg and Her Daughters, near Little Salkeld, are visible from Nine Standards Rigg. I subsequently visited both circles but on each occasion the horizons were too hazy to see the Rigg. It remains, however, that if in general people don't regard the cairns as ancient they won't investigate the possibilities with any thoroughness. If they had been in a circle instead of a line would they have attracted more attention? But the ridge is too narrow to accommodate a circle of such large proportions. So spiritualists, historians, archaeologists and scientists alike have ignored them, perhaps in the hope that they would go away.

---

2 www.ninestandards.eu

NINE STANDARDS

A few of the Nine Standards – Mickle Fell on the far horizon.

How relevant are the Nine Standards to the county boundary? It has been suggested that at one time it passed through them, the belief being that they were on the watershed. In fact they are some distance further north and even at the time of the Lyell-Hothfield Dispute the boundary did not incorporate them. But here's an interesting point; if they are indeed ancient they might well have existed when the boundary first originated, whenever and however that came about, and in view of the difficulties already referred to in determining its precise delineation would it not have been obvious to choose them as boundary markers regardless of their relationship to the watershed?

How about the theory, admittedly already dismissed, of under-employed shepherds indulging in a bit of spare-time building work? If this really were the case then given the size of the Nine Standards there must have been a fair number of them and they must have had a lot of spare time – seems unlikely. But let's examine another locality. Melmerby Fell, an undulating plateau between Hartside Top and Cross Fell, has large expanses of stony ground so there is no shortage of building material – and there are cairns everywhere. They put me in mind of a scene from *Planet of the Apes*. Although not rivalling the Nine Standards in size, many are carefully built and in some cases show symmetry in their arrangement while others are more random. But there are so many of them that they are quite useless as boundary markers or direction indicators; they would only cause confusion. So what is their purpose? Why are they here in such numbers? How old are they? I don't know.

Why are the Nine Standards so called? The number varies from time to time; beware of imitations, although the additional ones which occasionally appear are quite distinct from the originals. Dr. Walker mentions that in many old documents 'standards' appears as 'standers', or similar, and may be derived from the term used by miners to describe the columns of rock left in place to hold up the roofs of the galleries from which the mineral ores had been extracted.[3] It's interesting to note that there is a hill in Lunedale called Standards. It overlooks Fish Lake and Close House Mine, it is visible all over the area and it too has cairns on its summit, although they are tiny; even the most prominent one, which is actually a small shelter, is in no way comparable with the Nine Standards. I asked the Wemmergill keeper if he knew the origin of the name but he was unable to help.

So these mysterious monuments pose a lot of equally mysterious questions; I can only leave it to the experts to search for answers and return to more practical matters.

If you are up on Nine Standards Rigg, especially in good weather, you are unlikely to find it deserted. Many people will be tackling Alfred Wainwright's Coast to Coast Walk and they will automatically assume that you are doing the same. So when I was there attempting to trace the boundary down towards Beck Meetings I was constantly being asked which colour route I was following. (For those who may be unfamiliar with this part of the Coast to Coast there are three alternative colour-coded routes to Ravenseat, blue, green and red, for use at different times of the year in an attempt to minimise erosion). I spent a lot of time explaining what I was really doing and why. The Americans, of whom there were quite a number, the Coast to Coast being very popular with them, hadn't a clue as to what I was talking about – 'But we thought we were in Cumbria County!'

'Well, yes, you are in a way, but...' I pictured them sitting in the lounge at Keld Lodge that evening.

'Had a good day?'

'Swell, thanks. Met a guy who was walking some old boundary.'

'Gee, we met him too! Funny little guy in a big hat!'

---

[3] Walker, Stephen – *op. cit.*, 2008.

'Yeah, us too! Seemed to know a lot about these parts – told us how best to get here!'

'Took our photo for us up by those big heaps of stone! Said the stories about them were a lot of crap!' And so on…

However, dropping back down towards Kirkby Stephen I met two English ladies who asked me what the bogs were like. As there had been a lengthy dry spell I replied that they were fine. Then came the usual question of where I'd been. I told them.

'And are you going to write anything about it?' one of them asked.

'No, no,' I answered, 'it's just for the experience of it.' (I think I actually said either fun or hell rather than experience – I leave you, the reader, to decide which term you think the more appropriate).

And later – in fact several days later – I thought: 'Why not? Why not write something about it? It deserves it. And so does William Palmer.'

The result is this book. So if you two unknown ladies happen to be reading it – well, you've only yourselves to blame!

I've said plenty about the Pennine bogs already and it should be evident that wet peat will not be able to withstand the constant passage of thousands

Nine Standards Rigg on a good day showing the eroded peat before the slabs were laid.

of boots without suffering extensive damage. Bill Cowley, the originator of the Lyke Wake Walk, acknowledged that he had created a monster when the previously little-trodden route across the widest part of the North York Moors became a broad, muddy highway. The Coast to Coast has suffered the same fate around Nine Standards Rigg, to the extent that in early 2016 the North Pennines Area of Outstanding Natural Beauty launched an appeal to raise funds to lay stone slabs across the worst stretches.

In February 2017 I attended a presentation by Alastair Lockett, Field Officer with the Area of Outstanding Natural Beauty Partnership, illustrating the project; the financial target was surpassed and the work was nearing completion, to be followed by the adoption of the track as a right of way. There is now a super, sinuously curving flagstone path across the bogs around the head of Near Grains, with a new signpost indicating the red and blue Coast to Coast routes. There is also a smart new county boundary stone; this in time will weather down to tone in with those much older stones which have served to mark the line for centuries. Unfortunately it is inscribed 'Y/C' rather than 'Y/W'.

Some people disagree with this paving policy, claiming that it detracts from the wildness of the uplands, reducing the element of challenge, and they have a point; but when things get to a stage where a route becomes almost impassable and possibly dangerous (people have had to be rescued on occasions, and remember my own misfortune on Sleightholme Moor), something has to be done or the inevitable result will be constant widening of the track to avoid the bad bits, thereby exacerbating the problem. And in laying the slabs we are only doing what was done in previous centuries.

Many years ago I helped to excavate one of these ancient 'trods' which had recently been discovered near Robin Hood's Bay and I found the experience exhilarating and exciting – to walk where no-one had walked for generations, to think of those who originally laid the stones, who knows when, and those who had travelled that way and why. I might – just might – have got excited even if it had been a Roman road! The trods were a practical solution then and have proved to be so in our own time – think of how sections of the Pennine Way used to be. The task, as with so much in countryside management, is to strike a balance between what should be left alone, what could perhaps be improved and what is absolutely necessary, and knowing where to draw the line between them. I would hate to see slabs laid anywhere on the 'North West Frontier', even below Mickle Fell or along the Judgment Line. I do hope that between us William Palmer and I are not going to create another monster...

Thousands of people worship the great Wainwright; I am not one of them. Nor was the leader of a Lake District walk in which I took part a few years ago who didn't have a good word to say about him. My attitude towards him, as I've already hinted, is ambivalent. I have some of the books he wrote in collaboration with the photographer Derry Brabbs; these I read and enjoy but I've never used his guide books and never will. While I support the idea of making the Coast to Coast a National Trail, which would hopefully mean better maintenance, I've walked parts of it only because they coincided with where I wanted to go. To his credit, Wainwright devised his itineraries, as did William Palmer, without the benefit of present-day user-friendly Landranger and Explorer maps, now of a much higher standard and clearly showing rights of way and Open Access land. In those days the OS's authoritarian pronouncement that the inclusion on its maps of roads, tracks or paths was no evidence of rights of way applied to all thoroughfares, which was bound to lead at some point to conflict with landowners over access, so Wainwright is to be complimented on his persistence.

One would expect that as a long-term resident of Westmorland and a senior local government officer of the old regime Wainwright would decry the 1974 changes and indeed he does. In the introduction to *Westmorland Heritage* he says he has 'little sympathy' with them.[4] And his disapproval is not confined to Westmorland; in *Wainwright on the Pennine Way* he describes the River Tees as the boundary between Yorkshire and County Durham.[5] Although his choice of words is much less abrasive than mine I can only say 'Good on you, A.W.' But the account in *A Pennine Journey* of his passage through Weardale is, in my opinion, insulting and offensive,[6] to both the dale and those who lived there at the time and by association to those who live there today. It is not the Weardale described by Palmer, who explored it long before Wainwright and knew it far better (I said I would defend County Durham). We all have our opinions and prejudices of course, and it should be crystal clear by now that I have mine. I will leave it at that.

---

4 Wainwright, Alfred – *Westmorland Heritage, Popular Edition*, Westmorland Gazette, 1988.
5 Wainwright, Alfred – *Wainwright on the Pennine Way*, Michael Joseph, 1985.
6 Wainwright, Alfred – *A Pennine Journey: A Story of a Long Walk in 1938*, Michael Joseph, 1986.

Nine Standards Rigg to Aisgill Summit – the Mallerstang Valley

Looking upwards from the Keld-Nateby road at Hollow Mill Cross the descent from Coldbergh Edge, south of the Nine Standards, looks relatively quick and easy but the view is foreshortened and deceptive. From the top the location of the road is invisible unless there is traffic on it. There is no indication of the boundary line which must be determined from the map. The initial descent is steep, with rocky outcrops, and even where the slope eases the ground is rough and hummocky and there are fenced areas (with gated access). Tracks can be picked up which tend to lead to a wooden bridleway signpost by the roadside but this is a short distance north-west of the true boundary. Further still to the north-west, overlooking the road's steep descent towards Nateby, is the airy plateau of Tailbrigg Hill.

This, Palmer says, was his overnight camping site. To the east is the glacial valley of Dukerdale, a miniature version of the better-known High Cup on the East Fellside near Dufton. Tailbrigg is mis-called 'Tailbridge' by the OS, an example of its occasionally unsuccessful attempts to use local names on its maps – everyone in the Kirkby Stephen area knows it as Tailbrigg. The Dorrington Committee of 1892, set up 'to inquire into and report upon the present condition of the Ordnance Survey', reiterated the principle that the OS should adopt names commonly used by local residents even if such names were 'etymologically incorrect or suspect'.[1] However, a comment made by Mike Parker, author of *Map Addict*, in a 2016 BBC documentary *A Very British Map: The Ordnance Survey Story*, appears to contradict this. He said that the surveyors, in enquiring about place-names, were instructed first to approach the 'learned' classes – clergymen, schoolmasters, doctors, etc. – and were not to believe the people actually born and bred in the area, i.e. the common people, in fact the very ones most likely to know not only what a place was called but why. This instruction can still be found in the historical section of the Ordnance Survey website.

---

1 Owen, Tim and Pilbeam, Elaine – *Ordnance Survey: Map Makers to Britain since 1791*, Ordnance Survey, 1992.

The highest point on the North York Moors is Botton Head on Urra Moor. On early OS editions it appears as 'Burton Head'. The story goes, and I don't know how true it may be, that a cartographer, seeing it recorded as 'Botton Head' in the surveyor's notes, tried to be clever, interpreted it as the vernacular version of Burton Head and 'corrected' it on the map. In fact the two versions are unrelated; the 'correction' was itself corrected many years ago.

In the past the Ordnance Survey may indeed have been a typically British institution – old-school-tie, stiff-upper-lip, military-based, strictly disciplined, controlled and inflexible – but despite all that, or more likely because of it, and through decades of hard graft, patient dedication and

Boundary stone near Hollow Mill Cross
– Hamlet of Birkdale, County of York.

unwavering attention to detail, the result has been the production of the world's finest maps, a perfect fusion of art and science. They are fascinating, entertaining and informative, stimulating curiosity, thought and investigation. It's a contradiction in terms but I can lose myself in a map for hours on end. Long live the paper map! Down with computers, GPS, satnavs (Mike Parker calls them 'prat-navs'), smart phones and other such paraphernalia, all subject to battery failure, signal loss, water damage and other inconveniences which will always strike at a critical time! OS maps are not entirely infallible but if used properly they will rarely let you down.

A short distance along the road in the direction of Swaledale are two boundary stones, some yards apart. One reads 'Township of Nateby 1856', the other 'Hamlet of Birkdale County of York'. I was aware of their existence but not their significance until Stephen Walker told me that they are wrongly placed, overlapping into each other's territory, yet another example of the difficulties of defining such limits precisely. (At this point someone will no doubt draw my attention to the fact that such difficulties can now be overcome by the employment of the electronic and digital gadgetry lambasted above. They may do so if they wish – it makes not one jot of difference to me. Facebook means nothing to me and as far as I am concerned Twitter and tweet apply solely to the avian world. As for 'apps', I'm quite 'appy to be appless. Save the groans – there's more to come).

From Hollow Mill Cross the boundary climbs steeply up Careless Bank to High Pike Hill. There is a path but no fence to follow; however, it is safe to assume that the path and the boundary line are pretty much the same. It's not really important as the top of the climb reveals a fine prospect – the Mallerstang Valley. The boundary runs south above this spectacular and majestic dale through which the River Eden flows north towards Kirkby Stephen. Never was a river more appropriately named! The lower slopes of the valley are dotted with isolated farms while down below are the hamlet of Outhgill and the ruins of Pendragon and Lammerside castles and further north the historic Wharton Hall. Through its whole length runs the Settle to Carlisle railway, on the western side just above the valley bottom. The walk along the tops is straightforward, with no steep climbs, only a few areas which may prove boggy and a clear track.

Across the valley Wild Boar Fell appears as a craggy arête, although behind it is a large flat plateau. Its summit bears a number of cairns but they are much less impressive than the Nine Standards. It takes its name from

NINE STANDARDS RIGG TO AISGILL SUMMIT

Wild Boar Fell, Mallerstang.

the legend that the last wild boar in England was killed here in the fifteenth century by Sir Richard Musgrave of Hartley.[2] On his death Sir Richard was interred in Kirkby Stephen Parish Church. In the nineteenth century, following the collapse of the east end of the church, his tomb was opened and a boar's tusk was found inside. It is now on display in the church along with other curious items.

One interesting aspect of writing a book of this kind is that it has to be constantly revised and perhaps parts of it completely rewritten to incorporate new information and it is sometimes surprising how such information comes to light. I had always considered that the fifteenth century was too early a date for wild boar to have been hunted to extinction. I am writing this paragraph having, I thought, completed the book, but – and this has happened quite by chance – I have just read a chapter in the late Roger Deakin's *Wildwood: A Journey through Trees* describing his experiences of Oak Apple Day in the Wiltshire village of Great Wishford and the neighbouring Grovely Wood. In it he says that the manor and forest were bought by Sir Richard Grobham in 1603, describing him as 'an enthusiastic hunter

---
[2] Robertson, Dawn, and Koronka, Peter, *op. cit.*, 1992.

who was to slay *the last wild boar in England in 1624*'.³ (My italics). Whom are we to believe? I incline to the view that 1624 is a more probable date; but it's rather like deciding which place among several claimants is the centre of Britain or which is the country's oldest pub. Our opinions on such matters are often coloured by partisanship and you can't have failed to notice a great deal of that in these pages!

The cairns on Wild Boar Fell, and the view south along Mallerstang.

When lit by the morning sun the Mallerstang Valley is a fabulous sight. It is worthwhile to drop down from the boundary path as not far below are the rocky outcrops of Mallerstang Edge and Hangingstone Scar from where it is possible to see the valley floor, presenting an almost aerial view of the entire dale. Any words used to describe it are clichéd but it really is breathtaking. By now you will have guessed that I like Mallerstang, and I am not alone; Edmund Bogg says: 'the look out… is so fine as to beggar description… once viewed [it] is never forgotten.'⁴

In his recent Channel 5 series following his own coast to coast route Sir

---

3 Deakin, Roger – *Wildwood: A Journey through Trees*. Penguin Books, 2008.
4 Bogg, Edmund, *op. cit.*, 1909.

Tony Robinson, as a newcomer, declared that he preferred the Eden Valley to the claustrophobic atmosphere of the overcrowded Lakes – I'll second that any day! – and that he would certainly be returning.

On a clear day in any season it would be an exhilarating, if strenuous, walk to do the full round of the valley for both sides are equal in grandeur, but we must return to the task in hand.

Heading south, the highest point on the ridge – it's not really a ridge, more of an elongated plateau – is High Seat, followed by Gregory Chapel. No-one seems to know the origin of this name – there is no evidence of any sort of chapel – but it is mentioned in documents as far back as the seventeenth century. Next comes Hugh Seat, sometimes called in older references Hugh Seat Morville. No doubt about how this one got its name; Hugh de Morville was one of the knights who in 1170 took Henry II at his word and murdered Archbishop Becket in Canterbury Cathedral. This lofty ridge is believed to have been one of his favourite places. It must not be mixed up with Hugh Seat Nab near Tan Hill, mentioned earlier, although both refer to the same Sir Hugh. Many places in the Pennines have the same or similar names, leading to confusion for those unfamiliar with the local geography. Nearby is a marker stone inscribed 'AP 1664'. This is known as Lady's

Hell Gill Force, Mallerstang.

Pillar, the Lady and AP being the redoubtable and remarkable Lady Anne Clifford, Countess of Dorset, Pembroke and Montgomery, of whom more shortly.

There is now once more a fence to follow, which leaves the ridge to swing west, leading down to Hell Gill Beck. Palmer advises descending on the Westmorland side, describing the other as 'steep even for a sheep track'. I walked this section in the reverse direction, climbing up Hell Gill on the Yorkshire side, and it is indeed steep, with a lot of awkward little side valleys to negotiate, and there's no path. Descending leads to Hell Gill Bridge and a broad track known as the High Way. This is a long-established route, an old drovers' road which may also have been used by the Romans. Today it is a spectacular high-level walk, coming up from the head of Wensleydale, over the steep climb of Cotter End and along the upper slopes of the valley before dropping down to Outhgill and heading towards Kirkby Stephen.

A few miles south-east of Hell Gill Bridge is the ruin of High Dyke, once a drovers' inn. Whenever I pass it I think of what it must have witnessed, what tales it could tell of the great droving days when vast herds of

The ruins of High Dyke, once a drover's inn on the High Way.

The Watercut, Mary Bourne's sculpture on the High Way.

cattle were driven down from Scotland to the markets of lowland England, using the elevated, lonely inn as a stop-over, amid magnificent surroundings. No doubt the drovers themselves were less concerned about the marvels of the landscape than with the problems of delivering their charges safely to their destinations and the worries of getting paid for all their efforts. Northwards, as the track begins its descent, is a much more recent feature, a modern sculpture by Mary Bourne called The Watercut, one of a number in and around the Eden Valley.

Geoffrey Wright says that at the base of the parapet of Hell Gill Bridge is a small stone marking the Yorkshire-Westmorland boundary.[5] I've searched for this on several occasions without success but the lower part of the wall is covered in moss and obscured by grass and nettles. Nor have I ever seen properly into the deep gorge of the beck as the parapet walls are quite thick and those like me who are vertically challenged are unable to lean far enough over to peer into the depths. Hell Gill also has associations

---

5 Wright, Geoffrey N., *op. cit.*, 1985.

with Dick Turpin who reputedly leapt the gorge to escape the law.[6] He got around a bit, did old Dick, but why didn't he use the bridge? Further down the beck, just before the substantial bridge over the Settle to Carlisle railway, is the attractive waterfall of Hell Gill Force.

The High Way is often known as Lady Anne's Highway in honour of Lady Anne Clifford, possibly the most celebrated individual ever to live in Westmorland and still revered today, over 340 years after her death. Lady Anne was born in Skipton Castle in 1590, the daughter of Lord Clifford, Earl of Cumberland, the owner of vast estates in Yorkshire and Westmorland. She was less than five feet tall but what she lacked in height she more than made up for in spirit, resolution and determination. Her father died when she was only fifteen, leaving his fortune to his brother and nephew, thereby disinheriting his daughter. Much criticism has been levelled at him for this but perhaps he had good reason, not wishing such a huge responsibility to rest on a teenage girl who might have fallen prey to unscrupulous guardians or advisers.

Anne Clifford married twice, neither marriage being happy or successful. Her first husband, Richard Sackville, Earl of Dorset, squandered his wealth right, left and centre and together with the entire English nobility from King James I downwards opposed Anne's determined and continuing efforts to gain her inheritance. Six years after his death she married Philip Herbert, Earl of Pembroke and Montgomery (remember this name and title), and chose to be known as Anne Pembroke, hence the initials AP on the Lady's Pillar. Their relationship was not helped when the Civil War broke out for her husband supported Parliament while she remained a staunch and loyal Royalist.

Finally in 1643 her legal battles paid off. Her uncle and his son died and Lady Anne took rightful possession of the Clifford lands including the castles of Skipton and Barden Tower in Yorkshire, and Pendragon, Brough, Appleby and Brougham in Westmorland. She became High Sheriff of Westmorland and after the end of the Civil War in 1649 she travelled north and spent the rest of her life rebuilding and restoring all her castles, churches and other buildings and became a renowned philanthropist, distributing alms to the poor and purchasing all her household requirements locally.[6]

She appeared to show some magnanimity in her generosity for one of those to benefit was a certain Elizabeth Atkinson of Mallerstang who it is

---

6 Robertson, Dawn, and Koronka, Peter, *op. cit.*, 1992.

The ruins of Pendragon Castle, Mallerstang.

believed was none other than the widow of the luckless Captain Robert Atkinson, instigator of the Kaber Rigg Plot, whom Lady Anne had described as 'my great enemie'.[7]

Lady Anne's indomitable spirit continued into her old age. During the Commonwealth, when Oliver Cromwell heard that she was restoring her castles (many castles had been 'slighted' following the Civil War to prevent future use as Royalist strongholds) he threatened to destroy them. Lady Anne retorted that as fast as he did so she would rebuild them yet again. Cromwell was impressed; she was allowed to go on with her work.

Lady Anne died at Brougham Castle in 1676 at the grand old age of 86 and was interred in St. Lawrence's Church in Appleby. Sadly her successors, the Earls of Thanet, had no wish to spend money on maintaining such a large and scattered number of castles and with the exceptions of Skipton and Appleby they were allowed to fall into disrepair.

Pendragon, being situated in the Mallerstang Valley, is worth an extra mention. Its association with Uther Pendragon, father of King Arthur, is

---

[7] Holmes, Martin – *Proud Northern Lady: Lady Anne Clifford, 1590-1676*, Phillimore & Co., 1975.

only legend; it is believed that it was built around 1160 by Hugh de Morville who lost it following his involvement in the murder of Becket. His descendants later regained it and it passed subsequently to the Cliffords, Lady Anne restoring it more than a century after its destruction by Scottish raiders. She spent lengthy periods there, travelling with a large retinue from Wensleydale via the High Way. What a journey it must have been, lumbering up the steep ascent of Cotter End in great heavy coaches. Lady Anne herself described passing over 'those dangerous roads'.[8]

Today, wooden marker posts along the High Way bear little etchings of Lady Anne looking out of her carriage window. In the late seventeenth century the Earls of Thanet partially dismantled Pendragon and the elements completed the destruction. In 1963 it was bought by the Frankland family who have carried out a great deal of stabilisation and conservation work[9] and although it is on private land it is once again open to the public – who are advised not to go inside! It is in any case clearly visible from the road.

Now you remember Lord Hothfield? Yes, of course you do. Hothfield is in Kent, so too is Thanet, so how did Kentish families come to own the Clifford estates in Westmorland? Well, the family trees of the English nobility are not arrow-straight, sky-reaching Lombardy poplars but gnarled and twisted oaks, with branches everywhere and a tendency to hybridise. A perusal of *The House of Clifford*, researched and written by Hugh Clifford, 13th Baron Clifford of Chudleigh (1916-1988), illustrates this clearly.[10] Chudleigh is in Devon – need I say more?

Lady Anne's daughter Margaret married John Tufton, 2nd Earl of Thanet, and in 1849 the last Earl died, leaving an illegitimate son, Richard, who was born in France of a French mother. He became a British subject and was made a baronet in 1851. His son Henry was created 1st Baron Hothfield in 1881 and it was this Henry who, with Captain Lyell, became embroiled in the dispute which led to the alteration in our county boundary. So there you have it. The Hothfield family still live in Westmorland but Appleby Castle, which was their main residence, was sold in 1962. It is now a conference and wedding venue and is open for guided tours.[11]

---

8 Wright, Geoffrey N., *op. cit.*, 1985.
9 Frankland, J. C. – *Pendragon Castle,* Hayloft Publishing Ltd., 2002, (information leaflet)
10 Clifford, Hugh (Lord Clifford of Chudleigh) – *The House of Clifford,* Phillimore & Co., 1987.
11 www.applebycastle.co.uk

Remember too that I said the unearthing of new information often comes about in surprising ways? Roger Deakin's *Wildwood* was loaned to me by a friend and on the face of it there is no connection between it and the subject matter of *this* book. And yet delving at random into its chapters I came across the story of England's alternative last wild boar – a pure coincidence. And it doesn't end there. Later in the same chapter Deakin says that in 1807 the Manor of Wishford and Grovely Wood were purchased by none other than the *Earl of Pembroke and Montgomery*![12]

Lady Anne's second husband, Philip Herbert, passed on the earldom to his son from his previous marriage so there is no direct link through the families between Great Wishford and Mallerstang; but – wild boars; the Earldom of Pembroke and Montgomery; 'A Journey through Trees'; the 'gnarled and twisted' family trees of the nobility; so many coincidences, and all coming right out of the blue! I find it quite remarkable.

Returning to the boundary we cross the railway bridge and in a few yards reach the road at Aisgill Summit where there are cottages and bungalows but as far as I am aware no accommodation. The route now lies to the west, climbing up again onto the moors; but before that we must say a little about the Settle to Carlisle line which, like the Tan Hill Inn, has achieved iconic, even legendary, status.

---

12 Deakin, Roger, *op. cit.*, 2008.

Aisgill Summit to Rawthey Bridge

In the year of '69 they planned to run a train
From Settle to Carlisle all across the mountain range;
They employed three thousand navvies to build this mighty road
And across the fells through Appleby that old steam engine rolled.

And it's up in the morning, lads, in wind, snow and hail,
Hold fast to your hammers, lads, and lay another rail.

So wrote the Skipton-based folk singer Mike Donald a century after the event. Mike sadly passed away many years ago at the early age of 41 but his *Songs of the Broad Acres* live on. I was given the album as a leaving present when I quit my job as a bureaucrat to take up more useful employment and the first verse and chorus of *The Settle to Carlisle Railway* are reproduced here by kind permission of Mike's family.

The Settle to Carlisle line is the only regular means of public transport to operate anywhere near the 'North West Frontier' since Cumbria County Council in its infinite 'wisdom' withdrew subsidies for bus services, putting an end to the Kirkby Stephen-Sedbergh route along the Rawthey Valley. With careful planning the stations at Garsdale and Kirkby Stephen, though some miles from the boundary, can be used to access the Mallerstang area.

As mentioned in the bibliography there are many books about the line and it would be superfluous to go deeply into its history here but a comparison with the Stainmore line is called for. Like the Stainmore line it was a massive engineering and construction project, in a similar uncompromising, unforgiving landscape, under similar hostile conditions. Like the Stainmore line its completion was a triumph for the entrepreneurs who planned it, the engineers who designed it and the navvies whose back-breaking toil constructed it. Although it somehow survived the Beeching axe in the 1960s, like the Stainmore line it was subsequently subjected to a process of closure by stealth.[1]

---

1 Abbott, Stan and Whitehouse, Alan – *The Line That Refused To Die*, Leading Edge Press and Publishing, 1990

AISGILL SUMMIT TO RAWTHEY BRIDGE

It wasn't really stealthy at all, being obvious to everyone, but the methods were the same – running down the services, closing the small rural stations, inflating the costs of repair and maintenance – you've heard it all before. But unlike the Stainmore line it attracted the attention of a highly-motivated, well-organised and determined bunch of people who were fully prepared and well able to take on the powers-that-be.

The Friends of the Settle-Carlisle Line turned the closure proposals to their advantage – 'Come and travel on this historic line, it may be your last chance!' They were unexpectedly aided by the British Rail bureaucrats themselves who scored a spectacular own goal in appointing Ron Cotton as manager. Charged with overseeing the closure procedure Mr. Cotton in fact did exactly the opposite, promoting the line in any way he could and encouraging the public to use it.[2] Passenger numbers soared, to the dismay of British Rail who were forced to increase services. It was shown that the cost of repairs to the Ribblehead Viaduct, the principal reason put forward for closure, had been grossly overestimated.[3] In the face of public pressure and mounting evidence that they had got their figures wrong, British Rail's case crumbled and eventually fell apart. In 1989 the decision of that well-known railway enthusiast Michael Portillo, who just happened to be Minister of Transport at the time, banged the final nail into British Rail's closure coffin – the line was saved.

Since then it has gone from strength to strength. Friends of the Settle-Carlisle Line and the Settle to Carlisle Railway Trust work hard to promote the line and preserve its infrastructure. Particularly relevant to this book are the year-round programmes of guided walks organised by Friends of the Settle-Carlisle Line and Friends of Dales Rail; these start from all the stations along the line and have proved very useful to me in exploring the western side of the Pennines.

The line unfortunately suffered a major catastrophe in early 2016 when the appalling winter weather caused a colossal landslip, closing the section between Armathwaite and Carlisle in one of the least accessible places along the whole route. Re-opened at the end of March 2017, after a mammoth engineering project, it is once again in full operation and thriving.

Garsdale Station merits an additional word. From here it is possible to reach the east side of the Mallerstang Valley via the High Way, follow the

---

2 settle-carlisle.co.uk
3 Abbott, Stan and Whitehouse, Alan, *op. cit.*, 1990.

boundary north to Kirkby Stephen and return by train. Or do it in the opposite direction. It's a long way but it's worth it. Alternatively the west side can be accessed via Grisedale – I'll come to that shortly.

Garsdale was formerly known as Hawes Junction; the line along Wensleydale through Hawes joined the Settle to Carlisle line here. This line closed over a long period from the 1950s onwards but determined efforts by enthusiasts have re-opened it from Redmire eastwards to Northallerton. The ultimate aim of the Wensleydale Railway Association is to reinstate the entire line from Redmire to Garsdale; I wish them luck but I fear I shall be

Statue of Ruswarp, the heroic and faithful Border collie, on Garsdale Station.

pushing up the daisies long before it happens. (Have I said that before)?

Stories about the Settle to Carlisle are many, some true, some legend, some pure fancy. They can be found elsewhere but one deserves to be retold here, at least briefly, because it appeals to railway buffs, animal lovers, walkers and just about everyone else and it's true. It's the story of Ruswarp, The Dog Who Saved The Line.

Ruswarp (pronounced 'Russup', after the village near Whitby) was the inseparable canine companion of Graham Nuttall, co-founder of Friends of the Settle-Carlisle Line and its first secretary. When a petition was launched against closure Ruswarp added his paw print to the thousands of signatures. British Rail howled in protest (pun intended); but Ruswarp was a fare-paying passenger and it was ruled that he was entitled to record his opposition,[4] thus ensuring more publicity for the anti-closure campaign and becoming The Dog Who Saved The Line.

In January 1990, less than a year after the line's reprieve, Graham and Ruswarp travelled by train to go walking in the Welsh hills. They never came back.

They were not found until April. Graham, sadly, was dead. Ruswarp, though desperately weak and emaciated, was still alive. The story, as they say nowadays, went viral. Ruswarp survived long enough to attend Graham's funeral but passed away soon afterwards. At least he and his master had lived to see the line saved. Now the faithful dog's bronze statue sits on Garsdale Station, his eyes fixed on his master's memorial bench on the opposite platform. 'Garsdale', says the Friends' information leaflet, 'was their favourite place'. And Ruswarp also gazes towards the hump-backed ridge of Swarth Fell and it is there that we are heading next.

Like that from Hollow Mill Cross to Coldbergh Edge the view from Aisgill Summit to Swarth Fell is foreshortened. A field gate by the boundary signs on the roadside leads to a quad track which makes this uphill stretch relatively straightforward until it peters out when the steeper slope near the top is encountered. But it's not far and soon a cairn on Swarth Fell's southern outlier, Swarth Fell Pike, is reached.

Not a particularly remarkable cairn to look at but a very important one. So far we have been following the North Riding's boundary with Westmorland; but here its place is taken by that of the West Riding which, coming up from Garsdale, runs north-west then west, over the Howgills to our final

---

4 Abbott, Stan and Whitehouse, Alan, *op. cit.*, 1990.

destination on the River Lune. Meanwhile the North Riding turns south-east to accompany its western counterpart into Garsdale then far across the rest of the Dales uplands to the flat farmlands of the Vale of York and the outskirts of Yorkshire's capital city. What history and secrets does this boundary hold? Put it on the to-do list…

Swarth Fell Pike – the 'triple junction' cairn where the North Riding, the West Riding and Westmorland meet – Baugh Fell in the background.

In anticipation of undertaking this future adventure you can get a small taster by heading from Garsdale Station, across the A684 and over the soggy rise of Garsdale Low Moor into Grisedale. A short climb leads to the wall along the boundary between the Ridings; it's then a couple of miles to the triple junction cairn on Swarth Fell Pike. There, you've made a start! Now all you have to do is turn round and aim for York… but better to finish the current business first.

Grisedale, like Ravenseat, a hidden valley which once boasted a much larger population, was the subject of a documentary and a book by Barry Cockroft, the Yorkshire Television producer who 'discovered' Hannah Hauxwell. He called it *The Dale that Died*.[5] Having read the book I paid

AISGILL SUMMIT TO RAWTHEY BRIDGE

West Riding-North Riding boundary stone and milestone below the railway bridge, Garsdale Head.

my first visit to Grisedale in 2010. I found that reports of its death had been exaggerated, at least to some degree. I fell into conversation with the one remaining farmer in the dale who advised me to take the book with a pinch of salt. Even so, it appeared to me that Grisedale was hovering somewhere between life and death. A few buildings had been renovated and turned into holiday lets but several others lay abandoned and in some cases derelict.

A photograph in the book, taken in the 1960s or 70s, shows the former occupant of the most isolated and least accessible farm, Round Ing, standing before its crumbling walls. Round Ing is now just an area of broken and flattened stones with only the remnants of a wall. Grisedale has no Coast to Coast Walk, but a visit today shows that it is 'hanging in there'. And people, albeit a different kind of people, still need these out-of-the-way places. Life changes and while such places will never again be as they were, the changes help them to survive.

---

5 Cockroft, Barry – *The Dale That Died*, Dalesman Publishing Co., 1975 (included in *A Celebration of Yorkshire*, Dalesman/Yorkshire Television, 1989

From the triple junction cairn the boundary climbs up to Swarth Fell along a wall. 'Swarth' is derived from the Norse *svartr*. There is a waterfall in Iceland called Svartifoss; it flows over black basalt columns. Remember Upper Teesdale where similar dark igneous rocks occur and where you may have forded Swarth Beck? *Svartr* means black and under grey and threatening skies some of these Pennine heights look very black indeed.

Ahead is Wild Boar Fell but the wall swings left and a stile in the adjoining fence takes us to the head of Uldale Gill and the descent towards

The Cross Keys Inn, Cautley.

Rawthey Bridge. Palmer advises descending well out on the fellside; I advise it too, and keeping on the Westmorland side (the Yorkshire side entails a long detour to avoid an area of non-Open Access land). The upper reaches of Uldale Gill are innocuous enough but lower down there is the troublesome side valley of Grain Gill and lower down still, where it becomes Needlehouse Gill, the stream is rocky and the valley sides are excessively steep, partially wooded and potentially hazardous. The boundary runs along the gill but below Needle House it is impossible to follow it directly. A

The view north-east along the Rawthey Valley.

bridleway crosses it between Uldale House and Needle House; this is a good track and a branch to the right leads to Rawthey Bridge. Here the boundary turns to follow the River Rawthey; the A683 runs close to it, reaching the Cross Keys Inn at Cautley in a mile or so. But don't expect alcoholic refreshment here – it's a temperance inn! Here I had my first taste of 'Victorian' lemonade, produced by a well-known Tynedale firm – wonderful stuff!

Rawthey Gill rises on the slopes of Baugh Fell (it's pronounced 'Boe') and flows in an arc, north-east then north-west and finally south-west as the River Rawthey towards Sedbergh (it's pronounced 'Sed-ber' or perhaps by older people 'Sebber'). Backtracking from Rawthey Bridge along the bridleway then heading up the valley of Rawthey Gill makes a circular walk back to Grisedale but it can be a frustrating route. I followed it a few years ago in the opposite direction on a blazing hot day in July. It was frustrating because west of Grisedale the path hardly exists on the ground and passes through extensive areas of long grass and tall reeds, very trying for someone like me who is short on height, which combined with the heat and swarms of flies made it seem more like the African bush. It was also exhausting

The upper cascades of Cautley Spout, highest above-ground waterfall in England.

and on reaching Cautley I emptied my water bottle over my head. At times like this, or the opposite, when cold winds are blowing or rain approaching, when it's as lonely as it's possible to get in Britain and when it's miles back to civilisation, I ask myself: 'Why am I doing this? Why am I slogging it over all these bleak moors?' I answer immediately: 'Because I bloody well love it!'

Rawthey Bridge to the River Lune – the Howgills

An anachronism, an anomaly, an enigma – despite the tongue-twisting epithets the Howgills in their way are all of these. A triangular-shaped block of rolling fells sandwiched between the Cumbrian mountains and the Pennine hills but belonging to neither, they are a place apart. Although part of the Yorkshire Dales National Park (more of that shortly) they are geologically quite unlike the rest of the Dales. Made up largely of Upper Ordovician and Silurian siltstones and mudstones and a hard sandstone, the Coniston Grit, they predate the Carboniferous rocks of the Pennines by some 100 to 150 million years. In this respect they show more similarities with parts of the Lake District while retaining a distinct identity. The resistance of the rocks to weathering has resulted in broad, steep-sided, rounded hills separated by deep valleys, rather than spurs, arêtes or crags[1] (Cautley Crag is an exception).

Wainwright likened them appropriately to a herd of sleeping elephants – there, I'm not entirely anti-Wainwright! (Oh dear! Apologies to all connected with that much-loved Yorkshire-based television series *Last of the Summer Wine – that* pun *wasn't* intended but I've left it in because I like it. For the uninitiated, and I can't believe there are many, Aunty Wainwright was a character in the series played by the excellent Jean Alexander). But back to the Howgills – they are separated from the Pennines by the Dent Fault, the effect of which is clearly seen along the pass followed by the A683 from Sedbergh to Kirkby Stephen, particularly north of Rawthey Bridge where the landscape opens out and there is less tree cover. On the left the Howgills present smooth, steep, grassy hillsides while on the right are the exposed limestone pavements and rocky edges typical of the Dales.

The difficult landscape means the Howgills have no roads or settlements and few archaeological sites in the interior (again Cautley has an exception). They were never enclosed and are grazed as common land. Free-roaming

---

1 yorkshiredales.org.uk

Fell ponies – a frequent sight in the Howgills although these are in the North Pennines near High Cup.

fell ponies are frequently seen. Thus it seems that apart from the standard walking guides most books about the Howgills deal primarily with the periphery, concentrating on the Lune Valley, the villages of Ravenstonedale ('Russendale') and Tebay and the small town of Sedbergh. These are fascinating places of course, and well worth exploring, but strictly speaking they are outside the scope of this book, being located well away from the boundary. Howgill is a small hamlet on the western side of the massif. The Ordnance Survey adopted the name to cover the whole area, which was previously un-named. It too has Norse roots, *haugr* meaning hill and *gil*, a ravine. Given the nature of the landscape the name is fitting, although calling them the 'Howgill Fells' is tautological, 'fell' also meaning hill.

Now we must turn our attention to another boundary. From Tan Hill we have been following not only the county boundary but also that of the Yorkshire Dales National Park as it was designated in 1954. At that time it cut right across the middle of the Howgills, excluding all the land to the north; the Mallerstang Valley and its western approaches were also excluded. There was not a scrap of difference between the areas on either side of the boundary except that the excluded parts were in Westmorland – another piece of bureaucratic fudging which long ago lost any shred of relevance it might once have had. For many years there had been a campaign to change this anomalous situation and eventually official moves were made to extend the Yorkshire Dales National Park. A public inquiry was held in June 2013; I made two attempts to attend and missed it on both occasions, entirely through my own carelessness.

The local councils all raised objections to the proposals, claiming that business expansion would be stifled by extra planning regulations and that increases in property prices would penalise young local people unable to afford to remain in the area. These objections are perhaps not groundless but I suspect the principle reasons lay elsewhere.

There are a number of wind turbines on the fells around the Lune Valley. The efficiency of these visual monstrosities may be questionable, their intrusive and negative impact on the landscape certainly is not. Inclusion in a national park would scupper plans for further such schemes in the area concerned and the local authorities feared that communities would miss out on the... er, benefits which the energy companies claimed would be

Herdwick sheep – a traditional Lakeland breed but seen here in the Howgills near Cautley.

Summit of The Calf, highest point in the Howgills

forthcoming if developments were to go ahead.

Be that as it may, the inquiry report lay on a bureaucrat's desk for over two years when suddenly in October 2015 the extension was approved, no doubt to many people's surprise, certainly to mine. It came into effect in August 2016, making the Yorkshire Dales the third largest national park in Britain after the Cairngorms and the Lake District (which also received two small extensions; the Lakes and the Dales are now separated only by the width of the M6 and the West Coast main line). The procedure had taken some nine years.

Some local residents also have misgivings about the implications of the extension. Shortly after it came into effect I conversed with a farmer near Hell Gill. He wasn't exactly hostile to the idea but neither was he wildly enthusiastic. His attitude seemed to be 'we'll have to wait and see'. Meanwhile the people of Westmorland have once more asserted their independence, and rightly so, by holding a Westmorland Dales Day.

Over the last 60-plus years the Yorkshire Dales National Park has become a brand name and it would have been a mistake to change it; but it is entirely justifiable that the inclusion of parts of Westmorland should be publicised, particularly as it can be argued that places like Orton Fell, the northern Howgills and the western side of Mallerstang are not only outside Yorkshire but are outside the Dales too. No doubt the debate will continue for years to come. No matter how hard politicians and bureaucrats try in their pursuit of globalisation they cannot destroy people's sense of identity.

To return briefly to the Ordnance Survey and its autocratic, military-based governance, in 1920 Osbert Guy Stanhope was appointed as its first Archaeology Officer. He was treated with disdain by the organisation's hierarchy who regarded his work as superfluous and irrelevant to the main purpose of the OS. Even so he stuck patiently to his job for some 25 years and contributed much to the inclusion of archaeological information on OS maps. His comment on snail's-paced bureaucracy was that 'trying to get a move on in the Civil Service... was like trying to swim in a lake of glue.'[2]

As further proof of officialdom's procrastinating, and with particular reference to the Howgills, let's go further back, to the reign of Elizabeth I who, around 1584, issued a commission to enquire about the collapse of Rawthey Bridge and to take measures for its replacement. Some two years later she wrote expressing surprise at the delay in the execution of her former orders regarding rebuilding.[3] Even Good Queen Bess couldn't make headway! Plus ça change, plus c'est la même chose...

This will be my last tirade against the bureaucrats (I promise); but when I hear or read in the news that 'the Government/NHS/Foreign Office/DEFRA'... (insert whichever public body you wish here)... 'is committed to...' it makes me snort with derision. They say they are 'committed' but little seems to happen. Their stone-walling, in-denial arrogance infuriates me – 'This-is-how-we-see-it-we-know-it's-wrong-but-we-will-have-our-way-and-your-opinions-don't-matter.' I could go on but I'll resist the temptation.

There, I've done, and said tirade has brought us conveniently back to Rawthey Bridge; it is included on a list of bridges dated 1679;[3] whether it took nearly a century for it to be rebuilt I don't know but the present structure dates from 1820. From here the boundary follows the river for a mile or so then just before Cautley it swings north-west up the steep climb of Ben End.

Built in the early seventeenth century and considerably extended since,

---

2 Owen, Tim and Pilbeam, Elaine, *op. cit.*, 1992.
3 Hayes, Gareth – *Odd Corners Around the Howgills,* Hayloft Publishing Ltd., 2004

The rolling, airy ridges of the Howgills

the Cross Keys Inn was formerly a farm known as High Haygarth (Low Haygarth is close by). It became an inn in the early nineteenth century. At some time a member of the Buck family from Ravenstonedale, rather inebriated, was being helped homeward by the landlord; both fell into the river and were drowned.[4] In 1902 Mrs. Sarah Buck bought the inn and quickly sold it to Mrs. Edith Bunney who removed the licence.[5] In 1949 she willed it to the National Trust in memory of her sister on condition that it remained a temperance inn.[6]

Cautley is the last place on the 'North West Frontier' where accommodation may be found. Near the inn, steps lead to a footbridge over the river; on the other side bridleways go left and right. Turning right is our way to Ben End but first let's turn left. This may well be the most frequented path in the Howgills for it leads to Cautley Spout which can be seen in the distance, tumbling down its rocky ravine. This is the highest above-ground waterfall in England at some 650 feet but it is a cascade rather than a sin-

---

4 cautleyspout.co.uk
5 Mitchell, W. R. (Bill) – *The Lune Valley and The Howgill Fells*, Phillimore & Co., 2009
6 Hayes, Gareth, *op. cit.*, 2004.

The Howgills – Black Force, Carlingill – a fearsome scramble!

gle-drop fall. To its left is Cautley Crag, an impressive cliff face and the only one of any size in the Howgills. On the way to the Spout is an information board pointing out the site of an Iron Age settlement. It describes how a stone-edged causeway leads to the base of the falls and speculates that this place may have had some mystical significance for the people who dwelt here. Like High Dyke it's a spot which I can't pass without wondering what their lives must have been like. Pretty tough, I imagine.

Palmer suggests that anyone walking the boundary may prefer to take the path directly up the side of the falls rather than climbing up Ben End, but let's stick to the true route. It starts the ascent where Backside Beck joins the Rawthey a short distance upriver from the footbridge. There is a faint path but the slope is steep and tackling it on a warm summer's day I took it slowly and steadily. From somewhere to my left came the deep croak of a raven.

Pausing and looking back I thought I was being followed. I hadn't expected anyone else to be there and I was gripped by a quite irrational but compelling fear that this was someone walking the old county boundary with the intention of writing a book. Thinking about it now I can still feel just how strongly that fear took hold. I had to find out.

Reaching a point where the slope eased briefly I stopped and waited, on the pretence of having something to eat. I could now see that it was a man; he was moving much faster than I and it wasn't long before he came up to me. He was probably in his sixties and sweating profusely but looked very fit. After the usual pleasantries I tentatively asked him where he was going. 'Green Bell,' he said, to my intense relief. Green Bell is to the north-east and far from the boundary. I think I may have commented on his speed.

'I'm going Munro-ing next week,' he explained, 'and I need to get fit.' And with that he was off, hareing up the hillside like someone thirty or forty years younger. By the time I got going again, with suspicions allayed, he was way ahead and soon out of sight.

From the top of Ben End the boundary follows a wide curve left before dropping down to the col of Bowderdale Head. The slope is steep and although it is grassy it can be very slippery, and care must be taken not to swing too far left where some nasty screes are encountered. Then the best option is to take a narrow but level path towards Cautley Spout which eventually joins that coming up the side of the falls. Beyond the top of the falls this leaves the stream behind and continues across easier ground to reach a broad, firm track where turning right leads to the Calf, the highest point of the Howgills.

The Calf, at 2,220 feet, is, like Mickle Fell, a superb 360° viewpoint. Morecambe Bay can be seen and if the air is clear enough, Blackpool Tower. The Pennines, the Lakeland fells and even the Galloway hills range around the horizon. The Howgills themselves stretch away in every direction, long, soaring ridges separated by deep valleys. They may not be the highest hills in England but they strive hard to convince one that they are. This is walking country at its best! And not just walking – this is also excellent mountain-biking and fell-running terrain and the updraughts sweeping up from the dales make it perfect for paragliding.

From the Calf a grassy track, boggy in places, heads north over Hazelgill Knott and West Fell; on the right is Bowderdale, as wild and deserted as any Scottish glen, and on the left Langdale, which if anything is even wilder. Heading south, the broad track falls and rises over the Calf's neighbours, Bram Rigg Top and Calders – there is little difference in height between the three – and then sweeps south-westwards before descending to Sedbergh. This is an absolute belter of a walk – get out there and do it! The low-level return to Cautley is different but just as enjoyable, with views across and along the Rawthey Valley.

I started exploring the Howgills in the early 1990s and for some long-forgotten reason I limited myself to one visit a year; for several years I didn't go at all, being involved with other matters. There is thus still much to learn about them – it's on the to-do list. Then in 2005 I was training for a major trek in Africa and I reckoned that the steep hillsides of the Howgills would give my legs a thorough work-out, not so much going up as coming down – they knock hell out of your knees. So having climbed up to the Calf via Cautley Spout I headed to Calders then across country towards Cautley Crag intending to come down alongside Pickering Gill. I'd done it before and it's a terror. It was a beautiful day and in the distance I could see a man coming towards me accompanied by a German Shepherd dog. He appeared to have a badge or logo on his jacket and I thought he might be a countryside ranger. As he drew nearer I was concentrating more on his jacket than on him and I didn't really notice his face.

'Glorious day, isn't it?' he said as he passed.

'Yes, it is,' I replied, and I'd taken no more than two steps further when I thought: 'That was William Hague!'

Carlingill Beck near the bridge.

I didn't stop; I guessed that if it were Mr. Hague he would be quite happy not to be recognised on his day off. He is now Lord Hague, of course; so if he should be reading this and I've got it wrong then, Sir, I apologise. But I'm sure I wasn't mistaken.

Leaving the Calf the boundary heads north-west across Bush Howe, Wind Scarth and Docker Knott. Not far to go now! There is no fence or other indication of the boundary line and as elsewhere in the Howgills good map-reading is essential; the ridges and dales all look much alike and there are few distinctive landmarks. On one occasion I met a local lady, thoroughly familiar with the area, who told me she had once encountered poor visibility and had descended into entirely the wrong valley.

From Docker Knott there is another steep descent to Blakethwaite Bottom from where a path leads north down Uldale to the hamlet of Gaisgill in the upper Lune Valley; an alternative is to climb again up to Uldale Head and similarly go north over Hare Shaw and on to Tebay. But the boundary turns roughly west down Carlin Gill, the sting in the tail, the most difficult stretch of the entire route.

To avoid a long walk-in from Cautley or Tebay, over ground already covered, I decided to tackle Carlin Gill from west to east, heading up the valley from Carlingill Bridge. Knowing it would present some problems I looked online for route descriptions and advice. I found several but none was entirely satisfactory; some appeared to contradict others and there was no obvious 'best way'. The only thing was to go and see for myself. So

Carlingill Bridge.

having arranged an appointment at a nearby animal rescue centre to collect a new feline companion (Wainwright liked animals too) I set out to fill in some time by exploring Carlin Gill.

In recent years the toll taken on my knees by more than half a century of bog-dodging, stream-fording, rock-hopping, scrambling and the like has become at times painfully noticeable; worse, my agility and sense of balance have seriously deteriorated and with them my confidence on steep, loose ground, which is why throughout this book I seem to have emphasised the need for care on some of the slopes and stream crossings. Heading up the south bank of Carlingill Beck, making my way over awkward little rocky outcrops along a steep bankside with at best an intermittent path, I was soon aware that to complete this last stretch in safety I was going to need some back-up. With my appointment to meet my new cat in mind I retraced my steps to the bridge.

A week or two later, with cat having comfortably settled herself in by reorganising the house to her satisfaction, I returned with reinforcements – Grahame and Ray, both accomplished regular walkers. Crossing this time to the north bank we made good initial progress but the path gradually petered out and we became involved with the screes opposite the long cascade of Black Force. The ground was very steep, the path now almost non-existent. This led to some argument about how best to proceed. Grahame suggested we follow the sheep. 'They know where they're going,' he said. But on this sort of ground four cloven hooves are better than two flat feet; the safest way was to head uphill and traverse above the screes. The climb was so steep we had to use our hands but we made it and suddenly we were on easier terrain at the head of Uldale. We climbed again, up a less severe gradient, onto Uldale Head.

Grahame and Ray, who had never been there before, were impressed with the magnificent view but less so with the swarms of midges which conspired to interrupt our lunch. Pressing on across the flattish ground towards the head of Weasel Gill, from where we descended to the bridge, Grahame tripped over a blade of grass and executed a spectacular rolling tumble which carried him several yards. He was unhurt but Ray's request for a repeat performance for filming purposes was refused. Back at the bridge we discovered that although we had travelled less than five miles it had taken us nearly four hours and feet, ankles and knees were feeling the strain. As to whether we followed the 'best way' we were no wiser than when we set off. Grahame commented: 'There is no proper route – you make your own.'

W. R. (Bill) Mitchell (1928-2015), who edited *The Dalesman* for some twenty years, was the author of many books including *The Lune Valley and The Howgill Fells*. This contains a photograph of a Yorkshire-Westmorland boundary stone which he says was deliberately defaced during World War II.[7] The photograph appears to be taken somewhere near Carlingill Bridge. Like that at Hell Gill Bridge this stone has evaded my searches. Bill Mitchell's book was published in 2009 but the photograph is his own and could be of any date; the stone may no longer exist. If anyone knows

---

7 Mitchell, W. R. (Bill), *op. cit.*, 2009.

differently I'll be pleased to hear. Just to the south is Gibbet Hill where the bodies of Scottish cattle thieves were displayed as a warning to others. The minor road, Fairmile Lane, comes up from the south following the course of a Roman road to the site of a fort at nearby Low Borrowbridge.

South of Carlin Gill, Hole House is the reputed birthplace in 1456 of Roger Lupton who founded Sedbergh School in 1525. It is haunted by the ghosts of a woman and a black slave boy who were killed by the woman's husband in a violent fit of temper.[8] And here I must impart another snippet of information which I discovered by pure chance. Browsing in one of Sedbergh's bookshops I found a booklet entitled *Dr. Roger Lupton 1456-1540*.[9] The authors, Richard Cann and Elspeth Griffiths, state that Dr. Lupton's actual birthplace is unknown because there was more than one branch of the family, with one branch living at Hole House, Cautley. As former members of the staff of the school they should be in a position to know.

Below the bridge Carlin Gill for some reason becomes the much less attractively named Lummers Gill. The valley along these last few hundred yards of the boundary is deep, rocky and thickly wooded but a path runs down through bracken to a large stony outwash fan where the beck joins the River Lune – the end of the 'North West Frontier'! From here Yorkshire's boundary runs south towards Sedbergh, Ingleton, the Forest of Bowland, Craven, the South Pennines… an adventure for the future – put it on the to-do list!

---

8 Ffinch, Michael – *The Howgills and The Upper Eden Valley*, Robert Hale Ltd., 1982
9 Cann, Richard and Griffiths, Elspeth – *Dr. Roger Lupton, 1456-1540*, Sedbergh and District History Society, undated (possibly late 1990s/early 2000s).

Conclusion – Putting it all Together

Our trek along the 'North West Frontier' is over – what have we achieved? What have we learned? What has it done for us? And where do we go from here? Let's deal with these questions one by one.

What have we achieved? Apart from William Palmer's little book and my own offering here I can find no publications describing this route. Nor is there any trace online of anyone's having done it – and these days people are quick to post their accounts and photographs on the several walk orientated websites available. So it would appear that at a time when new 'Walks' and 'Ways' and 'Trails' and 'Paths', official or otherwise, are proliferating widely it's something a little bit different. And it's satisfying to know that it's a significant challenge which has been met and overcome.

Carlingill Beck joins the River Lune – the end of the North-West Frontier.

Of course, many people will have walked parts of it but there seems to be no record of a walk along its whole length. After all, it's a boundary which no longer exists in its original form, or so the bureaucrats would have us believe. But by following it we have proved them wrong – like those who carried out the perambulations centuries ago we have contributed in a small way to its continuing survival and emphasised people's regional identity.

What have we learned? Personally, when I set out to research the boundary I didn't really know what to expect and it has been fascinating to uncover so much history. Ironically the one intriguing mystery which was at least partly responsible for setting the whole thing in motion remains unsolved – that funny little zig-zag near Tan Hill. So in that respect I've failed but you can't win 'em all and anyway there's been plenty more to make up for it. As for you, I hope that what you've read and discovered has been interesting and entertaining and that perhaps it's inspired you to go and find out more.

Which brings us to the question of where do we go from here? The area we have explored extends no more than two or three miles either side of a linear route – the opportunities for widening the scope of investigation are almost unlimited. And wherever you live there's a boundary near you – follow it, see what it has to offer. Despite the obvious physical obstacles the 'North West Frontier' is easy in one respect – most of it is Open Access land. Other boundaries will inevitably present problems involving private property and will be difficult to follow closely. But adaptation and compromise are always possible. Planning is part of the enjoyment!

So much for the practical; what about the aesthetic? What has it done for us as individuals, for our identity, for our sense of belonging, for our health and well-being, for our spirituality and for what folk singer Ewan MacColl, when writing of his own love of mountain and moorland, called *The Joy of Living*?

When referring earlier to the potential dangers which they may pose to the walker I said: 'The Pennines don't take prisoners.' In fact they do, but in a different sense; they seize your soul, grasp it, chain it to them, claim you as theirs and there's no escape.

I have been lucky enough to travel to some very remote and exotic parts of the world. I have walked and trekked among some of the highest and most majestic mountains on Earth; I have crossed deserts, penetrated jungles and visited distant cities with strange and diverse cultures. I've seen

CONCLUSION – PUTTING IT ALL TOGETHER

some amazing sights and had some amazing experiences. But at no time have I ceased to be captivated by the Broad Acres of God's Own County and I can say that, whatever the rest of the world may have to offer, there is nowhere to equal them. They belong to me and I to them and I'm proud that it is so.

Ada Elizabeth Smith was born in Haltwhistle in 1875. By the age of thirteen she was a published poet and in her late teens she travelled to Europe with an inquiring mind and spent some years there, mainly in Vienna, to gain experience and an insight into life with the intention of becoming a novelist as well as a poet. She returned to England, to London, in 1897, where her work began to gain acceptance.

Tragically her promising literary career would never come into full flower, for in the summer of 1897 her health began to fail. She returned to Northumberland where a long holiday on the coast improved her condition but she was not cured. She went back to the polluted and unhealthy environment of late-Victorian London; despite coming north again in October 1898 her illness continued to advance rapidly and she died in Newcastle in December of that year. She was only twenty-three.

Although her life was so short her poetic output was considerable. A little volume of her work contains over 80 poems dating from the early 1890s to shortly before her death, some penned in places such as Paris and Dresden.[1]

Now you may be wondering why, in a book devoted primarily to the wild uplands of Yorkshire, I am embarking on a long discourse about a young poetess from Northumberland. Well, you may have noticed that, born in 1875, she was only a couple of years older than William Palmer. Her love of the moorlands around Blanchland and Tynedale is evident in her work, mirroring that of Palmer for similar places.

In his later years William Palmer lived in London – in fact he is buried there – and had Ada Smith not been cruelly snatched away so early in life it is quite possible that, with a shared love of writing and of the wide open spaces of the north, they would have met. He certainly knew of her; it was a short reference to her in *Wanderings in the Pennines* that made me curious about her. He quotes some verses from her poem *In City Streets* in which she contrasts the miserable gloom of London with the fresh wild beauty of

---

[1] No editor or compiler named – *The Collected Poems of Ada Elizabeth Smith*, Mitre Press, 1950.

the moorlands:

> *Yonder in the heather there's a bed for sleeping,*
> *Drink for one a-thirst, ripe blackberries to eat;*
> *Yonder in the sun the merry hares go leaping,*
> *And the pool is clear for travel-weary feet.*
>
> *Sorely throb my feet, a-tramping London highways,*
> *(Ah! The springy moss upon a northern moor!)*
> *Through the endless streets, the gloomy squares and byways,*
> *Homeless in the City, poor among the poor!*
>
> *Oh, my heart is fain to hear the soft wind blowing,*
> *Soughing through the fir-tops up on northern fells!*
> *Oh, my eyes an-ache to see the brown burns flowing*
> *Through the peaty soil and tinkling heather bells!*
>
> *London streets are gold – ah, give me leaves a-glinting*
> *'Midst grey dykes and hedges in the autumn sun!*
> *London's water's wine, poured out for all unstinting –*
> *God! For little brooks that tumble as they run!*
>
> *Oh, my heart is fain to hear the shepherd calling*
> *Far across the hillside, gathering his sheep!*
> *Oh, my body's starved for lack of dew that's falling*
> *Soft on northern heather, when the world's asleep!*

In an appreciation published in *The Academy* on the 17 December 1898 and reprinted in *The Collected Poems of Ada Elizabeth Smith* (1950), J. L. Garvin said:

> When she wrote it she must have been thinking all the time of Blanchland Common, and its wide, cool, purple silence...
> She would have liked to be buried [there]... it could not be so she chose the old churchyard of St. John Lee [between Hexham and Acomb]. The day she was buried was just such a day as would have made her laugh and walk twenty miles with you. She was free of the northern moors... and able to endure being much alone with them in... the solitude that is accepted, not compelled. Her... verses are like things plucked up out of the

---

2 Garvin, J. L. – *The Academy*, 17 December 1898.

CONCLUSION – PUTTING IT ALL TOGETHER

soft earth with the moist soil still clinging to their roots.[2]

A kindred spirit then with William Palmer, and indeed with all of us whose joy it is to lose ourselves (figuratively speaking, of course, and in fact it is more likely that we find ourselves) in the beauty of that vast swathe of country which stretches from the North Midlands to the Scottish Border and beyond. Is there beauty there, in all those miles of bleak and often storm-bound heights? Undoubtedly there is – an austere, rugged, even savage beauty perhaps, but one which attracts us, compels us to return again and again to experience it, to breathe in its atmosphere and to savour the effect it has on us. If you, the reader, were not one of us when we set out on this journey I hope by now you will have joined us.

Perhaps we should let William Palmer have the last word:

> I have read every book on the Pennines within my reach. I am never the worse for adding to my knowledge. All sorts of difficulties have supervened; but none have extinguished my love and desire for the biggest, wildest and highest of the Pennines, the upper dales where curlews whistle and gulls wail, and the brightest of wild flowers may be found.[3]

---

3 Palmer, William T., – *op. cit.*, 1951.

Updates

Things change, sometimes quickly. While this book was in the course of publication two significant things happened.

I discovered, once again by chance, that the 2016 Explorer map incorrectly shows the Yorkshire Dales National Park boundary at Tan Hill coinciding with the present county boundary, thus eliminating the zig-zag with which you will by now be thoroughly familiar. When I pointed this out to the Yorkshire Dales National Park staff they were mystified – they knew nothing about it! It appears that someone, presumably at the Ordnance Survey, has made a mistake. I understand that the matter is being investigated but up to press I've had no feedback.

The second occurrence almost resulted in my abandoning the whole enterprise. In August 2018 an athlete from Harrogate named Ben Dave ran the entire circumference of Yorkshire – some 500 miles! I congratulate him – I can't run for a bus – but without wishing to detract from his achievement I have to say it was with considerable relief that I found he had run the post-1974 boundary which includes only nine or ten miles of the 'North West Frontier', omitting Mickle Fell, Lunedale, Stainmore, Swarth Fell and the Howgills.

The moral? Never imagine that everything is set in stone. Other things may change, may already have changed. The investigation goes on.

Reference and Bibliography

This list is far from exhaustive – books on the history of Yorkshire and the Settle to Carlisle Railway for example are legion. Those listed here are ones which I have found most relevant and helpful. Some I have possessed for many years and may now be out of print or there may be later editions. Others are available in public libraries, those at Northallerton, Carlisle, Penrith and Kendal being particularly good sources. Some publications will appeal to the general reader (that sounds condescending but it's not intended to be), others are more specialised. Many can point the way to further investigation and research on any particular aspect of the historic counties of Northern England. Happy reading!

Abbott, Stan and Whitehouse, Alan, *The Line that Refused to Die*, Leading Edge Press and Publishing, 1990

Bellamy, David and Quayle, Brendan, *England's Last Wilderness: A Journey through the North Pennines*, Michael Joseph Ltd., Penguin, 1989

Bibby, Andrew, *The Backbone of England: Landscape and Life on the Pennine Watershed*, Frances Lincoln, 2008

Bogg, Edmund, *The Wild Borderland of Richmondshire: Between Tees and Yore*, Popular Edition, 1909

Bord, Janet and Colin, *A Guide to Ancient Sites in Britain*, Latimer New Dimensions Ltd., 1978

Brown, Iain, *The North Pennines: Landscape and Legend*, Summary House Publications, 2006

Cameron, Kenneth, *English Place Names*, Batsford, 1996

Cann, Richard and Griffiths, Elspeth, *Dr. Roger Lupton, 1456-1540*, Sedbergh and District History Society, undated (possibly late 1990s/early 2000s)

Clifford, Hugh (Lord Clifford of Chudleigh), *The House of Clifford*, Phillimore and Co., 1987

Cockroft, Barry, *The Dale that Died*, Dalesman Publishing Co. Ltd., 1975 (included in *A Celebration of Yorkshire*, Dalesman/Yorkshire Television, 1989)

Deakin, Roger, *Wildwood: A Journey Through Trees*, Penguin Books, 2008

Earnshaw, Alan, *The Wear Valley Way*, Discovery Guides, Local History Series, 1983

Falkus, Malcolm and Gillingham, John (eds), *Historical Atlas of Britain*, Book Club Associates/Grisewood and Dempsey, 1981

Ffinch, Michael, *The Howgills and the Upper Eden Valley*, Robert Hale Ltd., 1982

Forbes, Ian, Young, Brian, Crossley, Clive and Hehir, Lesley, *Lead Mining Landscapes of the North Pennines Area of Outstanding Natural Beauty*, Durham County Council, 2003

Frankland, J. C., *Pendragon Castle*, Hayloft Publishing Ltd., 2002 (information leaflet)

Grant, Russell, *The Real Counties of Britain*, Virgin Publishing Ltd., 1996

Gregory, Roy, *The Cow Green Reservoir*, in Smith, Peter J. (ed), *The Politics of Physical Resources*, Penguin Education/Open University Press, 1975

Hanson, Neil, *The Inn at the Top: Tales of Life at the Highest Pub in Britain*, Michael O'Mara Books, 2013

Hanson, Neil, *Pigs Might Fly: More Dales Tales*, Dale Publishing, 2015

Hartley, Marie and Ingilby, Joan, *A Dales Heritage: Life Stories from Documents and Folk Memory*, Dalesman Publishing Co., 1982

Hayes, Gareth, *Odd Corners around the Howgills*, Hayloft Publishing Ltd., 2004

Hey, David, *A History of Yorkshire: County of the Broad Acres*, Carnegie, 2005, 2011

Hillaby, John, *Journey Through Britain*, Constable and Co., 1968

Hillaby, John, *Journey Home*, Constable and Co., 1983

Holmes, Martin, *Proud Northern Lady: Lady Anne Clifford, 1590-1676*, Phillimore and Co., 1975

Keynes, Simon, *Shires*, in Lapidge, Michael, Blair, John, Keynes, Simon and Scragg, Donald (eds), *The Wiley-Blackwell Encyclopaedia of Anglo-Saxon England*, 2nd edition, 2014

Mitchell, W. R. (Bill), *The Lune Valley and the Howgill Fells*, Phillimore and Co., 2009

Owen, Amanda, *The Yorkshire Shepherdess*, Sidgwick and Jackson, 2014

Owen, Amanda, *A Year in the Life of the Yorkshire Shepherdess*, Sidgwick and Jackson, 2016

Owen, Tim and Pilbeam, Elaine, *Ordnance Survey: Map Makers to Britain since 1791*, Ordnance Survey, 1992

Page, William (ed), *Victoria History of the County of York, North Riding*, Constable, 1914

Palmer, William T., *Odd Corners in the Yorkshire Dales: Rambles, Scrambles, Climbs and Sport*, Skeffington and Son Ltd., 2nd edition, 1944

Palmer, William T., *Wanderings in the Pennines*, Skeffington and Son, 1951

Parker, Malcolm and Tallentire, Lorne, *Teesdale and the High Pennines*, Discovery Guides, 1987

REFERENCE AND BIBLIOGRAPHY

Raistrick, Arthur, *The Lead Industry of Wensleydale and Swaledale: Vol. 1 – The Mines*, Moorland Publishing Co., 1975

Rawnsley, John E., *Antique Maps of Yorkshire and their Makers*, MTD Rigg Publications, 3rd edition, 1983

Readers' Digest, *Folklore, Myths and Legends of Britain*, Readers' Digest Association Ltd., 1973

Richardson, Sheila, *The Forgotten Man of Lakeland*, Mill Field Publications, 1997

Robertson, Dawn and Koronka, Peter, *Secrets and Legends of Old Westmorland*, Pagan Press and Cumbria Library Service, 1992

Rollinson, William, *A History of Cumberland and Westmorland*, Phillimore and Co., 1978

Stenton, Sir Frank, *Anglo-Saxon England*, Oxford University Press, 3rd edition, 1971

Timpson, John, *Timpson's England: A Look beyond the Obvious*, 1992 edition.

Timpson, John – *Timpson's Leylines: A Layman tracking the Leys*, Cassell and Co., 2000

Townend, Matthew, *Viking Age Yorkshire*, Blackthorn Press, 2014

Wainwright, Alfred, *Wainwright on the Pennine Way*, Michael Joseph, 1985

Wainwright, Alfred, *Pennine Journey: A Story of a Long Walk in 1938*, Michael Joseph, 1986

Wainwright, Alfred, *Westmorland Heritage*, Popular Edition, *Westmorland Gazette*, 1988

Walker, Stephen, *Nine Standards: Ancient Cairns or Modern Folly?* Hayloft Publishing, 2008

Walton, Peter, *The Stainmore and Eden Valley Railways*, Oxford Publishing Co., 1992

Watkins, Alfred, *The Old Straight Track*, New Edition, Head of Zeus Ltd., 2014 (originally published 1925)

Williams, Michael, *The Trains Now Departed*, Preface Publishing, 2015

Wright, Geoffrey N., *Roads and Trackways of the Yorkshire Dales*, Moorland Publishing Co., 1985

No editor or compiler named, *Collected Poems of Ada Elizabeth Smith*, Mitre Press, 1950

Useful Websites

Appleby Castle	applebycastle.co.uk
Association of British Counties	abcounties.com
Boundary Commission	lgbce.org.uk
Cassini Maps	cassinimaps.co.uk
Cross Keys Inn	cautleyspout.co.uk
The Dalesman	dalesman.co.uk
Friends of the Settle-Carlisle Line	foscl.org.uk
Friends of Nine Standards	ninestandards.eu
Game and Wildlife Conservation Trust	gwct.org.uk
James Keelaghan	keelaghan.com
Judith Owston	judychasartefacts.com
Kirkby Stephen	kirkby-stephen.com
Lunedale	lunedaleheritage.org.uk
Ministry of Defence (access)	access.mod.uk
Mike Donald	mikedonald.co.uk
Milestone Society	milestonesociety.co.uk
National Library of Scotland	nls.uk
Natural England	naturalengland.org
North Pennines Area of Outstanding Natural Beauty	northpennines.org.uk
Ordnance Survey	ordnancesurvey.co.uk
Swaledale Sheep Breeders' Association	swaledale-sheep.com
Stainmore Railway	kirkbystepheneast.co.uk
Eden Valley Railway	evr-cumbria.org.uk
Tan Hill Inn	tanhillinn.com
Teesdale Mercury	teesdalemercury.co.uk
Wensleydale Railway	wensleydalerail.com
Yorkshire Dales National Park	yorkshiredales.org.uk
Yorkshire Ridings Society	yorkshireridings.org
Yorkshire Boundary Society	yorkshireboundarysociety.wordpress.com

The Author

Terry Ashby is a native of the West Riding and a professional Yorkshireman. After studying law he worked in local government until reorganisation led to a move into private practice and later into the property profession. He is interested in the natural world and has a degree in geological and biological sciences. At one time a member of the Royal Institution of Chartered Surveyors, he is currently investigating the history of traditional farm buildings in the Yorkshire Dales. Fascinated by wild and remote places he has travelled widely in Britain, Europe, South America, North and East Africa, Central Asia and the Russian Far East. He now works as a volunteer on conservation and countryside management programmes in the North Pennines.

Pictured below, the other North-West Frontier – the author on the Karakoram Highway near China's border with Pakistan.